T0248165

ZEN

AND THE ART OF

DIGITAL

TRANSFORMATION

SARA TEITELMAN, MPH

ZEN

AND THE ART OF

DIGITAL

TRANSFORMATION

LEADING A **MINDFUL REDESIGN**
OF THE **DIGITAL ENTERPRISE**

WILEY

Copyright © 2025 by John Wiley & Sons, Inc. All rights reserved, including rights for text and data mining and training of artificial technologies or similar technologies.

Published by John Wiley & Sons, Inc., Hoboken, New Jersey.
Published simultaneously in Canada.

No part of this publication may be reproduced, stored in a retrieval system, or transmitted in any form or by any means, electronic, mechanical, photocopying, recording, scanning, or otherwise, except as permitted under Section 107 or 108 of the 1976 United States Copyright Act, without either the prior written permission of the Publisher, or authorization through payment of the appropriate per-copy fee to the Copyright Clearance Center, Inc., 222 Rosewood Drive, Danvers, MA 01923, (978) 750-8400, fax (978) 750-4470, or on the web at www.copyright.com. Requests to the Publisher for permission should be addressed to the Permissions Department, John Wiley & Sons, Inc., 111 River Street, Hoboken, NJ 07030, (201) 748-6011, fax (201) 748-6008, or online at http://www.wiley.com/go/permission.

Trademarks: Wiley and the Wiley logo are trademarks or registered trademarks of John Wiley & Sons, Inc. and/or its affiliates in the United States and other countries and may not be used without written permission. All other trademarks are the property of their respective owners. John Wiley & Sons, Inc. is not associated with any product or vendor mentioned in this book.

Limit of Liability/Disclaimer of Warranty: While the publisher and author have used their best efforts in preparing this book, they make no representations or warranties with respect to the accuracy or completeness of the contents of this book and specifically disclaim any implied warranties of merchantability or fitness for a particular purpose. No warranty may be created or extended by sales representatives or written sales materials. The advice and strategies contained herein may not be suitable for your situation. You should consult with a professional where appropriate. Further, readers should be aware that websites listed in this work may have changed or disappeared between when this work was written and when it is read. Neither the publisher nor authors shall be liable for any loss of profit or any other commercial damages, including but not limited to special, incidental, consequential, or other damages.

For general information on our other products and services or for technical support, please contact our Customer Care Department within the United States at (800) 762-2974, outside the United States at (317) 572-3993 or fax (317) 572-4002.

Wiley also publishes its books in a variety of electronic formats. Some content that appears in print may not be available in electronic formats. For more information about Wiley products, visit our web site at www.wiley.com.

Library of Congress Cataloging-in-Publication Data

Names: Teitelman, Sara J., author. | John Wiley & Sons, publisher.
Title: Zen and the art of digital transformation / Sara J. Teitelman.
Description: Hoboken, New Jersey : Wiley, [2025] | Includes index.
Identifiers: LCCN 2024038148 (print) | LCCN 2024038149 (ebook) | ISBN 9781394273287 (hardback) | ISBN 9781394273300 (adobe pdf) | ISBN 9781394273294 (epub)
Subjects: LCSH: Information technology–Management. | Business enterprises--Technological innovations.
Classification: LCC HD45 .T39745 2025 (print) | LCC HD45 (ebook) | DDC 658/.05–dc23/eng/20240925
LC record available at https://lccn.loc.gov/2024038148
LC ebook record available at https://lccn.loc.gov/2024038149

COVER DESIGN: PAUL MCCARTHY
COVER IMAGE: © GETTY IMAGES | BEACHMITE PHOTOGRAPHY
SKY10091250_111924

I'd like to dedicate this book to my late grandfather, Sidney, a wonderfully witty and intuitive man who proved you don't have to give up your humanity to be successful in business.

Contents

Prologue

My First Computer

I'd like to share a brief slice of the journey that led me to be sitting down to write these pages. Born in 1976, I was by no means a digital native. Growing up in rural Connecticut I remember having a motorized antennae on our roof to capture faraway signals from three or four "local" TV stations. I would wrap my little hands around a large plastic dial on an even larger plastic box and ever so gently manipulate it one way or the other, depending on atmospheric conditions, as the picture dimmed, brightened, and eventually solidified from so many black and white frenetic dots into a fully congealed color picture. I don't recall thinking at all about the technology that supported this process, much like I'm sure my six-year-old daughter doesn't give a thought to how her tablet, and the software it runs, operates.

My first real consciousness of technology, as we perceive it today (i.e. being synonymous with some type of device, usually a computer) was when my parents bought me an Apple IIc. This was a truly amazing piece of technology at the time – one of the first accessible desktop computers for mere mortals like me, an eight-year-old child who begged and pleaded ceaselessly until my parents shelled out the $1295 plus tax, along with some required floppy discs containing "programs," as we called them.

These programs were mandatory because, on its own, the computer's OS didn't really do much for those who couldn't code. There was *Apple Writer* for word processing, *Flight Simulator II* (which was frustratingly advanced), and of course, my favorite at the time, *Where in the World Is Carmen Sandiego?* The fact that I had only miniscule understanding of how my computer worked, and hardly any awareness of the multitude of things outside my eight-year-old self's

Apple IIc with monitor, circa 1984
Bilby / Wikimedia Commons / CC BY 3.0.

realm of interest, did not in any way stop me from being completely smitten with this little machine. And it was little! The CPU portion, which was integrated with a keyboard, weighed only seven and a half pounds. It even had a handle in the back, signaling the owner could grab it and take it along on a journey (although without the much heavier monitor, I'm not sure what good that would do!).

My use of this computer started off very simply. I couldn't wait to get home from school, run upstairs, fire up the IIc, hear the clicking and whirring of the floppy disc drive, and then dive into my game of choice from the welcome screen that slowly materialized before my eyes. While I enjoyed the experience, the inner workings of my little machine remained veiled behind the friendly interface of the programs. But one day, that changed.

Growing bored with the tame, safe environs of my games, I wanted to venture out of bounds, into the underlayment of the computer. I began flipping through the voluminous owner's manual that came with my IIc and stumbled upon a tutorial on how to use the programming language, Logo, to draw various shapes. Aha! Now I was on to something. Following the instructions, I quickly found myself in a completely different world. Gone were the pixelated graphics of my good friend Carmen, and in its place was a lonely, monochromatic, blinking cursor. This cursor filled me with wonder. And dread. Much like an astronaut experiencing the vastness of space for the first time, I was overwhelmed and in a complete state of wonderment. How could this innocuous little line on an otherwise blank screen be the entry point to a vast universe of computing resources and embedded knowledge?

And off my little fingers went, carefully reproducing each line of code from the manual until, at the final press of the "return" key, a perfect triangle appeared! Amazement, and more complex shapes, ensued. I was hooked.

The rest of the story about how I got from there to here is not exactly a straight line. One might guess from what I shared that I then went on to get a degree in computer engineering from Cal Tech, and then on to an illustrious career in tech. But that is not even close to what happened.

That ember of fascination at the possibility of harnessing the power of technology to create something from nothing burned low and slow in my little being. It would be many years (roughly 23) until I decided to turn my attention fully toward technology and its role as a tool for creation, human connection, and so much more.

Preface

"In the midst of chaos, there is always opportunity for growth and transformation."

– Zen master Daigu Ryokan

Welcome! I'm so glad you stopped by. Let me throw another log on the fire and make us some tea.

Before we dive into the matter at hand, please pause a moment. Close your eyes and take a few deep breaths. Think about the extraordinary journey that led you to this exact moment in place and time. It is no doubt intricate, beautiful, and yes, sometimes challenging. You are full of knowledge, expertise, and experience around a vast array of subjects. You are here now, reading or listening to these pages, because your heart and mind connected you with this book in some way. That means something. You are seeking information or guidance. You are evolving. And what an amazing opportunity that is! In every moment, new connections are made, and old ones broken. Life is constantly being reinvented. And so are we, individually and collectively, being constantly reborn into the next moment, and the next.

Now take a few more deep breaths. And with that, let everything remembered, your past feelings, concerns, and desires, wash over and through you like a nourishing rain. Feel the rain soak into your bones and become one with all that you are, solidifying your structure, but not weighing it down.

And now, here we are again, sitting by a roaring fire, having a cup of tea. Moment to moment we are changing, without fear, and without knowing or caring what is coming next.

It may seem a strange beginning to a book about enterprise technology. But hey, the act of transformation, whether digital or otherwise, requires an intense degree of clear-mindedness and a complete commitment to putting all preconceptions, fears, and prejudices to rest.

Only then can a new reality, in tune with the present moment, begin to emerge.

Thank you for being here. I will do my best to honor the precious time we will spend together and to share what I can to help you on your journey.

A Word on Zen and the Beginner's Mind

"In the beginner's mind there are many possibilities, but in the expert's, there are few."
                    – Shunryu Suzuki, Zen Mind, Beginner's Mind:
                    Informal Talks on Zen Meditation and Practice

If you're reading this book, you've probably been focused on improving the state of the digital workplace or enterprise technology for some time. And in this time, you've probably accumulated a lot of knowledge and experience about what works, and what doesn't.

In Zen Buddhism, there is a concept of beginner's mind or *shoshin*. The basic premise is that when your mind is empty and open, your ability to learn is at its peak. Much like children take in new information with a sense of wonder and discovery, anyone seeking to evolve beyond what they already know should approach every situation with fresh eyes. Approaching subjects in this way helps us to escape the trap of only taking in information that confirms previously held beliefs.

Without discounting what you know, I urge you to open your mind to the ideas and approaches in this book. Many may sound like things you've tried before. And in some cases, you may have been met with disappointing results.

As each "familiar" topic comes up in the chapters that follow, I ask that you notice what biases arise within you. For example, phrases like "That will never work" or "Been there, done that" may close the door to valuable reflection on how small adjustments to previously attempted efforts could transform their effects.

As you sit quietly with this book, take this opportunity just to listen. And in that listening, try to hear what your innermost authentic self is telling you, free of the tyranny of the intellect. What feels good and right? What doesn't feel right and why? What urges arise within you to act differently at the next opportunity? You will use this same open approach to listening as you discover, or rediscover, the technology-related experiences people are having across your organization.

You may find that some of the information presented is helpful and directly applicable to the situations you're facing, and that's great. The primary purpose of this book, however, is to create space for you to reflect on the ways in which your and others' relationship with workplace technology might be hurting us and contemplate what we can do to change that. It is not a foregone conclusion that we will remain victims of subpar technology tools and approaches forever. We have the power to change the difficult reality that most employees are experiencing in relation to the tools they rely on to get work done. That change starts with you.

PART I

Preparing for the Journey

Every successful journey starts with a period of thoughtful preparation. In this first stage of the digital transformation effort, resist the urge to rush out and buy what feels like the right technology solution. It's tempting to leap ahead, past the messy and time-consuming work of clearly seeing and defining the problems and root causes of the numerous difficulties plaguing our organizations. It is in our nature to be solutions oriented, and the companies wishing to drive our decision-making around major tech investments would prefer it that way.

The time for selecting the right tools will come soon. For now, be in the moment and really "sit" with the problems that you and the organization are facing. Know that the work ahead, while much harder than signing a contract, will pay off in ways not yet imagined. And when it comes time to commit to a particular set of solutions that will support new ways of working at your organization, you will be confident that this is indeed the path toward putting technology to its best and highest use, not just another "Let's hope it works out" Band-Aid approach.

CHAPTER 1

Applying Zen Concepts to the Digital Enterprise

Before we dive into the practical steps and methods that form the core of this book, let's briefly explore how Zen concepts can be applied in the context of digital transformation.

Zen is a school of Buddhist thought originating in India in the fifth century BCE that emphasizes the practice of meditation and mindfulness as a way of being in harmony with oneself and the world. One of Zen's main principles is to understand that there is no "I" or "you," that in essence, we are all one. By understanding this simple but profound idea, we will more easily be able to practice compassion and empathy and be of service to all humans. This is much in line with the modern concept of servant leadership.

Empathy is a concept I will touch on throughout this book, particularly in the early stages of the digital transformation journey. Listening and fully understanding the plight of employees across the organization during the initial discovery stages of the effort is one of many opportunities you will have to flex your empathy muscles.

Another key principle of Zen Buddhism is the idea that we exist in a state of constant change. From one moment to the next, every atom and particle is rearranging itself into an infinite variety of configurations and as a result there is no such thing as permanence. The Zen school of thought suggests that the illusion of permanence, whether of things perceived as external or internal to oneself, can only lead to suffering because change is an unavoidable reality. Only

3

when we release our attachment to the illusion of permanence, and our fear of change, can we achieve a more joyful, enlightened state.

The number one challenge digital transformation leaders will face is managing and supporting desired levels of change in the organization. As we'll explore later in this book, humans are naturally change averse. There is significant effort required to bring a population of people through a period of major changes without causing harm and giving rise to years' worth of negative repercussions. For this reason, we must take this aspect of digital transformation very seriously, not rushing through or overlooking anything that can be done to ease people through what will inevitably be an uncomfortable transition.

This may sound like heady stuff for a book on enterprise digital transformation. But consider for a moment some of the key reasons why organizations of all types and sizes are currently in a state of crisis when it comes to the ***digital workplace*** – the collection of digital tools that people use to perform their work.

Employees are Feeling Frustrated and Disengaged Due to the Overwhelming Number and Complexity of Digital Tools they Interact with Day to Day

Workplace stress and burnout have reached epidemic proportions. A 2023 study from the American Psychological Association found that 77% of workers surveyed reported experiencing work-related stress, with 57% experiencing negative impacts including emotional exhaustion and lower productivity.[1] Interestingly, most reports on employee burnout, including this one, fail to mention technology as a contributing factor. Yet it's hard to imagine, even without strong data, how technology isn't in some way implicated.

Over the last 10 years, the number of applications that an employee must interact with to perform their work has risen significantly. In 2024, organizations with more than 2000 employees had an average of 231 cloud applications, representing a 67% increase from 2014, when the average was 77.[2] In many cases, these apps are not integrated, which leads to information silos that can require employees to spend inordinate amounts of time manually moving data across disconnected systems. Compounding the inherent challenges with tech overload are unsanctioned applications – unofficial subscription-based software-as-a-service (SaaS) that have overrun organizations like an invasive species. People's natural propensity for solving problems with shiny new objects, combined with aggressive SaaS marketing and incentivized viral adoption, have resulted in a perfect storm of out-of-control subscription costs, chaotic IT landscapes, and deeply frustrated end users. A 2023 survey of 743 IT professionals found that 59% of professionals were finding SaaS sprawl a challenge, with 65% of SaaS application unsanctioned.[3] The rise of unsanctioned apps, often referred to as "shadow IT," presents significant security risks as well. If IT is not actively managing a given application, it's impossible to enforce an organization's security and compliance policies for data residing in that system.

In this context, it is surprising that more attention isn't being paid in the digital transformation space to how organizations can streamline and downsize their tech stack. As we'll talk about in this book, digital transformation does not have to involve the addition of new technology. In fact, most organizations would benefit from a significant technology "haircut." Not only would this help address the challenges that employees face when jumping between several often separate but partially duplicative tools, but it can also result in significant cost savings and efficiency gains.

In addition to struggles related to the sheer number of tools, employees rarely receive adequate technology training and support, both at the time of their hiring and at regular intervals, leaving them struggling to make full use of highly advanced, constantly evolving technology. In a recent report by McKinsey, senior executives involved in digital transformation efforts cited talent as the biggest barrier to achieving their digital strategies.[4] As a result, the role of IT is shifting and expanding into areas once reserved for HR. It is not surprising that one study found that 80% of IT professionals reported taking on increased levels of responsibility for the employee experience, including work to support training and onboarding of new and existing staff.[5]

Even everyday tools, like those used for document or spreadsheet creation, are advancing at such a breakneck pace that regular users may be unaware of major features and functionality that could make their work easier and more enjoyable. Or worse, they begin to lose the ability to perform the basic operations that they had mastered in the past.

These trends are troubling but not surprising. Imagine putting a pilot who has been flying a single-engine Cessna for the last 15 years behind the controls of a state-of-the-art passenger jet with little to no instruction, and then telling them that their livelihood and professional reputation rest on their ability to routinely take off and land this foreign machine without incident. A healthy dose of anxiety would be expected. Yet this is the kind of situation employees are facing daily, with little to no empathy from organizational leaders, IT professionals, and the tech giants pushing the next greatest thing.

I am continually surprised by how little compassion is displayed toward the average worker when it comes to the challenges they face adapting to the ever-changing enterprise technology stack. Even when HR provides every manner of program to support other aspects of the employee well-being, people are often left hanging when it comes to their digital tools. I can't help but think this picture would look different if digital transformation took the time to truly empathize with what the average employee is experiencing.

Resistance to Change in the Workplace is Generally seen as Something to be Overcome, not Understood

As humans, we desire to be in control of our lives. Most of us accept that there are some things that fall outside of our control. But when it comes to our work lives, we prefer predictability. This is natural and expected. And yet time and again, organizations introduce highly disruptive technological change without acknowledging what a massive emotional toll this can take on the average worker. In fact, in my digital transformation consulting practice, I often hear the term PTSD (post-traumatic stress disorder) used in reference to past digital initiatives gone wrong. And of course, just like PTSD, every subsequent effort perceived as similar to past events incites the same or worse levels of fear and anxiety, which often go unnoticed or unacknowledged by leaders.

Many traditional organizational change management (OCM) approaches treat employees as empty vessels who can be manipulated using clever marketing techniques and authoritative leadership. Little attention is paid to the hopes, fears, and dreams of those who form the lifeblood of the organization. But what if there were? What new, co-created realities could emerge that would not only excite employees but propel them, and the organization, to new heights of productivity and worker happiness?

These are just a few examples of how concepts that have been carried through cultures and continents over millennia can serve us in the current age, where technological change is occurring at a rate that we can barely grasp, let alone keep up with.

This book is meant to serve as a practical guide to all those who, by choice or obligation, are looking to guide their organizations to use technology more responsibly, thoughtfully, and with a focus on the human experience. We will start by providing guidance on what it means to be a digital transformation leader, and to provide some tools to help you formulate your approach to bringing people together from across the organization in service to a common goal. Then we will transition into a discussion of the ideal digital workplace, and how the act of decluttering – eliminating redundant, extraneous or outdated technology – can free up the organization to deliver a truly enjoyable digital employee experience.

While this is a business book, not a spiritual text, I hope that the ideas it contains will inspire you to explore the connection between the ancient wisdom of Zen and other spiritual traditions and the now perpetual state of digital transformation that we find ourselves in. And above all, I hope that this book will help you to find and spark more joy and meaning in your workplace!

Your Assignment

◆ Have you ever tried meditating? If so, great! This one will be easy. (And if you're a regular meditator, you'll know it's not always easy!) In any case, sit in silence or with some relaxing music and begin by reflecting on your reasons for starting down this path. Review in your mind the events leading up to this decision, or at least the impulse, of leading your organization to a better place. Then as you reflect on these things, feel them melting away, into your heart, and then letting go of them altogether. Keep processing until you feel a sense of emptiness surrounding you. No expectations, no fears, no anticipation or nervousness, just pure potential. Remember this place and know you can come back to it anytime you wish – in a darkened room, on a Zoom call, in a brightly lit meeting room, driving in your car. It's always available to you when you need it.

CHAPTER 2

(Re)Defining Digital Transformation

We will begin by defining, or redefining, what digital transformation means for your organization.

What is it and what are we looking to achieve?

One thing we can say for certain is that digital transformation is not synonymous with introducing new technology to the organization. Anyone who has been part of a failed technology rollout can tell you that transformation – at least positive transformation – did not take place. In fact, many highly successful digital transformation efforts focus solely on making better use of the technology already in use, or even trimming it down.

So where does that leave us? If you're looking for a simple starting point, I've provided a definition of digital transformation for you to use (see below). To make it your own, read on for an overview of what I consider to be the core elements of digital transformation. By thinking more deeply about each of these elements, you'll be able to come up with a unique definition that perfectly aligns with your organization's culture and context.

> ***Digital transformation*** **is the process of aligning enterprise technology to user needs and business processes in ways that advance organizational culture and performance.**

Three Key Elements of Digital Transformation

Think of digital transformation as an actionable set of considerations for how technology is used in your organization. The elements listed below are intended to help you consider what digital transformation means, or can mean, to your organization. This is a great thought exercise for the early stages of a new technology-related project. You may even want to brainstorm ways in which the project you envision adequately addresses each element.

PURPOSEFUL

Technology that you deploy within your organization should be in service to the organization's values, mission, and strategies. First, start with what the organization is trying to accomplish, internally and externally, and examine the ways in which technology could speed progress toward desired goals and outcomes. That is where your digital transformation journey should begin.

HUMAN-CENTERED

To determine exactly how technology could better support your organization's goals and desired outcomes, deeply explore the human side of the equation. How is technology helping or hindering people's work? What could be done to increase productivity and, even more importantly, the overall quality of the employee experience? Freeing up staff time spent on routine tasks that could be automated, for instance, could unlock tremendous value for the organization while increasing worker happiness. Put another way, it's about honoring and creating space for what's uniquely human, while tasking machines with what they do best.

RESPONSIVE AND RESILIENT

Organizations, and the world at large, are not static entities changing at predictable intervals. They are living, constantly evolving, and highly complex systems that often change and morph in surprising ways (COVID-19 is but one recent example). No technology has an infinite life span, but platforms can be selected and configured in ways that are designed to nimbly weather and respond to change rather than break down or require intensive investments every time an adjustment is needed. If you feel constrained or "stuck" because of your current technology, you've already lost your competitive edge. It's time to make the leap.

Communicating effectively about digital transformation and what it means to your organization is the most important first step you can take as a digital transformation leader. Developing your organization's own definition is also a great way to get potential collaborators, champions, and gatekeepers on board and engaged at the beginning of your journey.

Hold a visioning session or lunchtime brainstorm. Have fun with it and start generating excitement about what's possible. And most importantly, set a collaborative and inclusive tone that will carry throughout the digital transformation process. Even if the digital transformation project is still more dream than reality, you'll be able to kick off a round of important conversations that can lead to a considered "go" "no go" decision.

The Ideal Versus Real Digital Workplace

The tangible goal of the digital transformation journey is to optimize the digital tools that employees rely on to get work done. This virtual work environment can be referred to as the *digital workplace*. Transforming the digital workplace can unlock huge potential for your organization.

> **Digital workplace refers to the technology people use to access, store, and share data, information, and knowledge at work.**

In an ideal digital workplace, a variety of technology platforms and tools work together to form a cohesive, user-centered digital ecosystem. Each tool has a specific and distinct purpose, which is well understood by all those who use it. Figure 2.1 provides a visual overview of some of the key components of an ideal digital workplace. While by no means exhaustive, it introduces a framework for

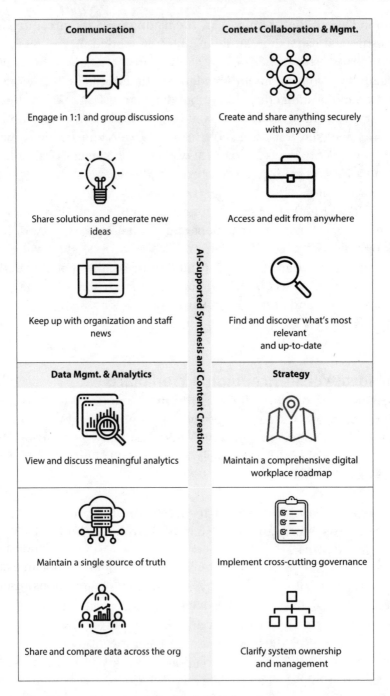

Figure 2.1 Key components of the ideal digital workplace.

thinking about the digital workplace as an organized and interconnected set of capabilities reflective of how an end user experiences their collection of digital tools.

Alas, the digital workplace at most organizations is far from ideal. As the state of enterprise IT has evolved, monolithic ERP (enterprise resource planning) systems and their relatively few satellites have gradually been replaced by a sea of fragmented technologies. While ERP systems may remain, they are often viewed as relics of a forgotten age, treated with care and respect but tiptoed around whenever possible to allow business to be conducted more efficiently.

These workarounds themselves give rise to inefficiencies and staff frustration. With departments and individuals making decisions regarding which shiny new cloud application will help them get work done faster and better (and they all promise this), the result is a confused mashup of tools taking root in different pockets of the organization, like unruly invasive species, growing virally and haphazardly.

This puts IT professionals in an uncomfortable, if not perilous position. Outside of highly regulated industries, they tend to lack the authority to issue sweeping edicts about which technology is "allowed," that is, unless they have the support of leadership. Awkwardly, it is often leaders who shepherd in new, shiny tools, and then require their staff to adopt them. In this scenario, IT staff are torn between letting staff use whichever applications they wish or instituting draconian, punitive measures to prevent the influx of unsanctioned applications.

The "middle way" is no better. Enforcing some rules around officially sanctioned systems, while letting others run free, creates an atmosphere rife with infighting, favoritism, and even clandestine efforts to bring in new tools to sideline existing ones. It's not an exaggeration to say that the IT landscape of some organizations resembles the plot of a *Game of Thrones* episode!

What is the net result of this digital chaos? The employees who generate the inputs and outputs of these various systems are left to suffer. Amidst the chaos, they must duck and cover while doing everything within their means to get work done on time and to expectations.

I will never forget one particular woman – let's call her Joan – at a prominent New York nonprofit who, during a focus group interview, broke into tears explaining her way of coping with the fact that their fundraising database and marketing CRM (customer relationship management) didn't talk to one another. Each quarter, she would export the entire database into Excel and review, line by line, 50,000 entries to ensure that the data was up to date. Our focus group was the first time she had shared this fact with anyone. She had been secretly performing this "fix" for more than six years and it was taking, by her estimation, at least 30% of her time. She was scared to tell anyone, for fear of being identified as the cause of the inefficiency.

The benefits of looking at the collection of digital workplace tools holistically and thinking how they can best work together are many. Perhaps top of mind for IT and organizational leaders is how changes can benefit the bottom line. In Joan's case, the source of the inefficiency would be properly identifying the source – the lack of integration between the CRM and the fundraising database – and then justifying the investment needed for integration by quantifying the cost savings to be realized through a massive reduction of staff time needed to manage data transfer between systems. By conducting these types of discovery and analysis activities across the digital stack, the organization can begin building a roadmap for how to significantly improve the state of its operations while cutting costs and reducing worker burnout (more on this later!).

Your Assignment

- ◆ Review your organizational strategies, IT strategies and plans, and other relevant documents while reflecting on the role technology could or should play in the near future to support achievement of the stated objectives and activities
- ◆ Develop a working definition of digital transformation specific to your organizational context. This could be in the form of a summary statement and series of talking

points. Or, if something slightly more formal is required, try your hand at a concept note that includes the following sections:

- Background: The organizational context or call to action for why the organization should take a more intentional approach to designing and optimizing its digital landscape
- Introduction: An organization-specific definition of digital transformation and scope of what will be covered under the proposed initiative
- Objectives: The aims of the digital transformation initiative, what it will set out to do and by when
- Expected Outcomes/Benefits: Detailed list of what will be realized if the initiative is successful
- Considerations: A list of prerequisites and potential risks that must be considered before moving forward with the initiative
- Next Steps: A list of actions or tasks that will help to build momentum for the initiative and get the right people involved from the start

◆ Begin sharing these ideas or concepts more broadly with colleagues. This could begin with informal conversations with members of your team and colleagues who you feel would be open or enthusiastic about the ideas presented. This will help build support and your sense of confidence about taking this work forward. (You'll deal with the naysayers later, once things have picked up steam!)

CHAPTER 3

Leading Differently

"A leader is best when people barely know he exists; when his work is done, his aim fulfilled, they will say: we did it ourselves."

– Lao Tzu

Whether it is your first or your tenth foray into digital transformation, this is a chance to start fresh. You are now on the path of serving those who will benefit most from any changes to your organization's use of technology: your employees.

In my consulting practice, I often observe a complete disconnect between leadership and staff when it comes to how technology is functioning (or not) for the benefit of the organization. Most leaders interact with enterprise technology in a very limited way. Email and document creation, sure, but when it comes to more complex tasks, it is common for an executive to request the needed product (spreadsheet, report, etc.) from someone else. This means they are often several steps removed from the reality that others in their organization are experiencing.

I have had CEOs tell me, without hesitation, that they are unaware of any major issues with their organization's commonly used digital tools. Meanwhile, I have just stepped out of a session where their staff were close to tears describing the effort it takes to produce a frequently requested report.

No one is at fault here. The executive simply sees what they see. And the employee fulfilling their request (just like Joan from the

17

previous chapter) is often too embarrassed or ashamed to raise the issue, thinking this will be a reflection on their own skills or work performance.

Leading differently in situations like these means being willing to look beneath the surface and see what's really happening – without judgment or blame, and with empathy for those who may be staying silent in fear of losing their jobs, or at least their reputations.

Here are 10 qualities you can cultivate to be a more empathetic and effective digital transformation leader.

1. **Believe in the change.** You should fully embrace and understand the need for and value of the envisioned change. Your passion and excitement will shine through in all that you do, and you'll easily ignite these same feelings in others through your authenticity.

2. **Help others believe in the change.** Take time with fellow leaders and employees (even the technophobes!) to build their understanding of the digital transformation project, how it will help the organization, and most importantly, how it will help them. Although your peers in leadership positions might have signed off on the project, they may not truly grasp its implications. They might also feel timid about asking questions if they don't feel digitally savvy. Empower them to own and feel comfortable with the effort, making it easy for them become collaborators and champions.

3. **Be collaborative.** Plan and execute each key step with input and involvement of people from across the organization. Sure, this will make things go a little slower, but it will pay huge dividends when it comes time to roll out changes to the organization. In fact, lack of meaningful collaboration is why many digital transformation initiatives are dead on arrival. Good intentions routinely get crushed under the weight of resentful colleagues who were left out of the process.

4. **Be empathetic.** Again, empathy! Make it a priority to understand people's needs, challenges, and desires from across the affected parts of your organization. Change efforts that overlook the importance of empathy in project planning and solutions design can have major adverse effects on employee

morale. Listen deeply and make sure that your effort is directly responsive to what you heard. Being a good listener is more than being quiet while others are speaking. It involves asking good questions – and sometimes hard ones – and then being open to considering viewpoints that differ from your own.

5. **Understand, then design.** Don't design solutions in a vacuum. Get out and see how people work. Understand the problems people are trying to solve. In some cases, the best way to understand is to simply observe someone performing a series of tasks. This "fly on the wall" approach can yield volumes of information that would never come out of an interview or focus group. Simply put, co-design a solution together with end users that truly addresses the problem as they see it, even if it differs from how you see it. This is one of the key tenets of human-centered design.

6. **Work openly.** Be comfortable carrying out your work openly and transparently. Make meeting minutes or summaries available to everyone. Create a suggestions/questions box. Share frequent updates, even when there have been mistakes or setbacks. Mistakes are inevitable in large change efforts, so own them and let others know how you're applying the lessons moving forward.

7. **Realize there are multiple ways to learn.** Accommodate the different ways in which people take in new information, from watching videos to reading short narratives to taking part in hands-on trainings. Ensure everyone has a solid start on using their new tools so they can fully embrace new ways of working without barriers.

8. **Be nimble and patient.** Understand that organizational change resulting from digital transformation is not a linear process and that it should not be rushed. Wherever needed, slow down to revisit your course of action, validate assumptions, and make necessary adjustments, especially when conditions within or outside your organization shift.

9. **Have fun!** Be sure to inject fun and creativity wherever possible, from games to launch parties with giveaways to producing fun video shorts or having users submit their own. Digital transformation can feel heavy and serious, so help

lighten the mood and make it fun for people to get involved and celebrate the new.

10. **Acknowledge yourself for doing the right thing.** If you're doing all – or even most – of the above, you're in the top percentile of digital transformation leaders! And no matter what, don't let the inevitable naysayers get you down. They are there to remind you to be humble and listen to everyone, even your biggest detractors, and that you should never stop upping your game for the benefit of all.

In addition to these core qualities, the key for digital transformation leadership is *resilience*. The path of transformation is rocky, with many ups and downs. There will be times when you question your logic for starting down this path. At other times, you'll be elated at how those abstract ideas from early in the process are coming to life and making real, visible changes in the way people work and interact. Throughout it all, stay grounded and don't let the extreme positives and negatives distract you from the ultimate goal.

For example, I have seen many digital transformation leaders fall into a deep funk after their first or third setback, throwing up their hands and deciding this isn't worth the trouble (who am I to rock the boat?). Remember in these times that you are doing this because you believe, and know in your heart, that things can be better. It's that unique passion and vision that you have, and can pass on to others, that is the spark that will keep this initiative alive. If you turn your back on it now, you'll be looking back years from now thinking about what might have been. Don't let the inevitable resistance to change extinguish your flame.

I've seen other leaders get so swept up in the excitement of it all that they have forgotten the true meaning of the work they started. For example, some may get completely wrapped up in a particular technology solution. Dazzled by the marketing literature and slick demos, they are convinced, much like a cult member, that this particular solution is the answer to everything. They begin bombing every technology-related discussion with not-so-subtle hints about how "if we just implement application XY, this would totally solve that problem" and other starry-eyed narratives. Not only will colleagues quickly become annoyed and disengaged, but the heart of the effort, the "why" of it all, will begin to slowly melt away. This is a fast way to lose the confidence of your collaborators, steamroll others' perspectives, and discredit what started out as a noble effort.

And if you're not feeling up to it after reading this chapter, don't dismay. Leaders, in my humble opinion, are made, not born. Qualities that you didn't even know you had will emerge and develop when needed. Fear not! It's that fire in your belly that will keep you charged up over the long haul. The rest will fall into place in time.

Practicing Human-Centeredness

"I think we all have empathy. We may not have enough courage to display it."

– Maya Angelou

Digital transformation can only succeed if it's human-centered. You can deploy cutting-edge technology, but if the solutions don't map to people's specific needs, or if you fail to properly support them through this change, that awesome tech will be dead on arrival.

In human-centered digital transformation, technology comes second to understanding the people and work processes that the technology will be serving. In other words, digital transformation should not be a solution in search of a problem. To design solutions that stick, start by listening. Then validate what you think you heard and listen some more. Understand the pain that people are experiencing around their work and never waiver from delivering the best solution to their challenges, even if it differs from what you thought you were going to do (or even what you were most excited to do!).

Human-centered approaches, which are embedded in every chapter of this book, are your secret weapon for ensuring that your digital transformation effort is a success. These approaches will help you effectively understand the need, mobilize champions, design user-centered solutions, and support a smooth transition to your ideal state.

The practice of human-centered design contains a variety of useful tools for defining and understanding the problems you are trying to solve. Here we give you a high-level overview of this important practice so that you can begin thinking about how to employ it from the earliest stages of your project. You will have a chance to start applying human-centered design later in this book as you set out to fully understand people's needs, hopes, and concerns related to their digital tools. These methods will continue to serve you during later stages of the project, as you validate assumptions and co-design solutions in close collaboration with others from across the organization.

Core Concepts of Human-Centered Design

Human-centered design and its cousin, design thinking, involve designing solutions for and with real people. It is a repeatable process that leverages design principles and human insights to develop creative ways to address *any* problem. Human-centered design involves an iterative problem-solving process built on four key principles:

1. **Solve the "right" problem.** Before getting to the work of designing a new approach, product, or service, you must understand the root problem you're working to solve. Often when we see a problem to fix, our limited experience points us to symptoms of a much larger issue, and we miss the real challenge that needs to be addressed. Finding and fixing the root problem by conducting research and talking to real people ensures that you spend time and resources wisely.

2. **Focus on the people.** Our society tends to be solution focused. What technology will we use? What will the product look and feel like? But without thinking of all the people who will be impacted by the solution, our designs end up flawed from the start. How many products can you think of that have flopped or been scrapped because people choose not to use them, or truly can't use them? It's critical to consider the people you are designing for and listen to their needs throughout the design process.

3. **Consider the entire system.** You cannot design solutions in a vacuum. When it comes to the digital workplace, every part of the user experience is interconnected. Focusing on just one process, such as onboarding, won't necessarily make the entire digital workplace experience better for new

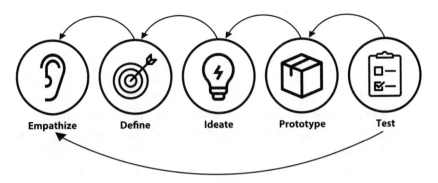

Empathize   Define   Ideate   Prototype   Test

Figure 3.1 The human-centered design process.

employees. Instead, as you define and design each component, always keep the big picture in mind. What do you want
your users to think, feel, and achieve with your final product
at every step of their journey?

4. **Iterate and validate design decisions.** No designer gets it
   right the first time. (And by employing this process, *you* are a
   designer!) You will be working with imperfect or incomplete
   information, especially as you work to bring human insights
   into the process. The most effective and efficient approach for
   creating a workable end product includes ideating and proto-
   typing a variety of solutions and <u>testing them with real people</u>.
   Figure 3.1 shows a typical human-centered design process.
   Note that each step has an arrow prompting you to revisit
   the previous step, as every new discovery should open space
   for re-evaluation of past thinking. Above all, it is important to
   remember that *you are not the end user*. Nothing can replace
   testing with real users to gain insights about what works, what
   doesn't, and what needs to be tweaked or redesigned.

Embarking on a digital transformation for your organization can
be an exciting endeavor but also potentially costly. Getting it wrong
can result in sunk costs, lost morale, and a diminished reputation.
Taking a human-centered approach can help alleviate the risk of
your transformation effort going sideways.

In any digital transformation, you're dealing with three key components: the business, the technology, and the people. Each of these

areas should be given relatively equal consideration, yet often the people get overlooked. By involving people outside the project team in the process from the very beginning, you're not only solving for the business impacts of your technology initiative, but also solving for pain points and challenges that real people face in your organization.

A human-centered approach has the added benefit of getting buy-in from across the organization and laying the groundwork for change to smoothly unfold. According to a McKinsey report on change management, "to feel comfortable about change and to carry it out with enthusiasm, people must understand the role of their actions in the unfolding drama of the company's fortunes and believe that it is worthwhile for them to play a part."[1] Asking for user input on the change that needs to be made, through interviews, focus groups, surveys, ethnography, co-creation workshops, and other tools for gaining insight, gives people an opportunity to have a stake in the proposed transformation and helps them see where they fit into the long-term vision.

Applying Design Thinking to the Digital Workplace

If we accept that many organizations have a fragmented digital workplace littered with redundant and disconnected IT systems, then what is the solution?

For that, we turn to someone whose methods have nothing to do with enterprise IT: Marie Kondo. If you haven't read her books, you are likely at least familiar with Ms. Kondo. She is the bestselling author of *The Life-Changing Magic of Tidying Up, Spark Joy,* and *Joy at Work*. The method she has developed, which she refers to as the KonMari® method, is as simple as it is revolutionary.

Her Netflix series, *Tidying Up with Marie Kondo,* features a binge-worthy parade of American households in dire need of tidying. Each episode begins with Ms. Kondo walking into a home where both the home and its inhabitants need help: random items and children's toys strewn everywhere, kitchen in disarray, closets stuffed, clothes overflowing in piles on floors and beds. The harried homeowners are at their wit's end, desperate to escape the chaotic nightmare they wake up to every day (not unlike the staff at many of my client organizations!). And then in walks Kondo, a petite, serene Japanese woman wearing cream-colored, perfectly pressed attire and a sympathetic smile.

Within minutes of TV time, she gets to work. But before diving into the actual job of tidying, she does something unexpected. She asks the owners of the house to sit down on the floor with her, close their eyes, and imagine their ideal lifestyle. She asks them what will be different about their lives once the tidying is accomplished. The goal, in other words, is not just a tidy house but a completely reimagined life. Once her clients allow their minds to envision this ideal future, all manner of hopes and dreams begin to surface: a more harmonious marriage, more time for my children, a healthier lifestyle.

When I saw this show for the first time (and I must admit, I was late to the Marie Kondo party), I had a flash of insight. For years, I had been running my consulting firm helping organizations with all manner of digital transformation projects. Usually the projects involve selecting and building one or more enterprise business applications. As part of that process, we always take a step back and employ some design thinking methods I had picked up during my time working in the international development sector, where human-centered design and design thinking became popular in the 2010s.

The first time I tried out design thinking, before I knew it by that name, was as a graduate student, studying public health at the University of Washington. My task was to help a village in rural Kenya define what local community development projects it should focus on and how they would be managed. I did this at the request of my friend, Loyce, who was born and raised in this village and now lived in the United States. While she didn't have a background in public health, she intuitively knew the right way to launch this ambitious effort and, to my surprise and delight, enlisted my help. As we discussed how we would approach the project, I introduced a method I recently learned of in my graduate studies: participatory action research (PAR for short).

The premise of PAR is that researchers, activists, and scholars can come together with communities to co-create solutions to their most entrenched challenges. As one paper puts it, "PAR is a collaborative, iterative, often open-ended and unpredictable endeavor, which prioritizes the expertise of those experiencing a social issue and uses systematic research methodologies to generate new insights."[2]

So off we went to Loyce's home village in western Kenya, which at the time had one of the highest rates of HIV infection in all of sub-Saharan Africa. Our first goal was to interview as many different groups and factions within the community as we could, to gather their issues and points of view. We spent several days conducting these meetings, from morning to night. We spoke with teachers from the local primary school, elderly men, mothers who had banded together to care for the numerous AIDS orphans, adolescents, and others. In each meeting, we would ask the same question: What would you like the future to look like when this community project is up and running? Not what do we need to *do* or *fix*. But how would life be better?

I witnessed immediately the magic of PAR, which I would later understand as a form of design thinking. Faces went from exhausted and dismayed to hopeful and energized as people described life in this hypothetical future. Orphans would have a quality education with a hot meal twice a day. Men would be able to produce goods that they could sell at market. Local farming would be revitalized. There would be a place in the village to receive basic healthcare and medicines. So many amazing ideas!

As Loyce and I sat with her mother at the end of each day in Loyce's childhood home and reflected on what we had heard, we were filled with joy. "If they can imagine it, all we have to do is to figure out a way to make it happen!" Naïve as it may sound, what this process helped us do was get out of the realm of problems, which were legion, incredibly sad, and overwhelming, and into the realm of dreams, intentions, and soaring spirits. That is the magic, and dare I say, alchemy, of design thinking.

■ ■ ■

As you embark on this journey, look for opportunities to dream big, unfettered by the current reality. Closely listen to what people have to say and you may be surprised by what visions of the future emerge. While we are concerned in this book with the realm of the digital workplace, do not lose sight of the fact that today's post-COVID world of work is, largely, a digital experience. With most organizations going hybrid or fully remote for the long term, we must think of their digital workplace as the community or landscape in which much of their workday is lived. For this reason, the realm of IT can no longer be relegated to those concerned only with whether a system functions as expected. It is now the job of every business leader to concern themselves with the quality of the digital enterprise.

Your Assignment

- Reflect on your personal leadership style and past performance and think about the ways they have served you and the efforts you have led. Write down the top three things you are most and least proud of and why. Then write down a five-point plan for how you will bolster your skills for the road ahead. This could include anything from reading a particular book to taking an online course or meditating 10 minutes a day – whatever you feel serves the purpose. There are no wrong answers.
- Connect with a trusted person in your life; this could be a friend, a partner or a spouse, or a longtime colleague. Explain to them the outlines of what you are seeking to do. Ask them to share their honest opinion about which of your qualities will help you succeed, and which of your qualities may give rise to challenges. As you do this, try to be as objective as possible, as if you were discussing someone else, not you, so as not to take it personally or feel hurt. This will be a great preparatory exercise for what's coming. Putting yourself out there as a leader will inevitably attract criticism and you'll have to be able not only to "take it," but to embrace it as an opportunity for self-expansion and understanding.
- As you begin down the path of this leadership journey, begin keeping a journal to help you reflect on, and keep some distance from, the experience. For instance, you could quickly jot down every few days the following bullets:
  - What I am feeling proud of – perhaps overt actions or just ways that you processed or responded to a particular event

(Continued)

(Continued)

- Where more work is needed – places where you felt you could have shown up differently or where the turmoil you experienced could have been avoided or lessened had you taken a different approach

♦ Reflect on your capacity for empathy. Some people seem to be natural empaths, highly attuned to the emotions of others. This isn't always a good thing, because you can become overwhelmed or easily set off balance by someone else's feelings and reactions. The practice of empathy that is part of the human-centered design process is somewhat different. This is an active state of listening that goes beyond the words you are hearing to begin reading into and feeling what it is like to be in that person's shoes. Once you feel closer to that person's experience, you can begin formulating approaches from an angle that is likely different from the one you would have taken in isolation.

♦ Try this out with a friend, colleague, or loved one who is sharing a challenge in their life. Instead of diving into a predictable flow of judgment and sense-making from your own perspective, put a pause on that impulse. Listen to what that person is saying, without your intellect or logic jumping in, and just try to feel what that person is experiencing – no judgment, no preconceived notions. Then, once you've listened, actively respond by empathizing. Statements like "That sounds so difficult, I'm sorry you're going though that" signal this to the other person.

♦ Then reflect on how that felt, especially if this feels different from how you would usually approach this type of conversation. What felt different, and how did the conversation that followed change compared to the usual?

♦ Keep practicing this skill in your daily life where you can. For many of us, empathy is a muscle that is not well exercised. This regular practice will go a long way in preparing you for the work ahead.

CHAPTER 4

Preparing the Way

Which scenario sounds better to you? In one, you rush ahead into the unknown, only to encounter unforeseen obstacles, lack of support, and a variety of other unpleasant surprises. In the other, you plan for and anticipate potential risks, fortify strategic alliances, and proceed well equipped for any challenge you may encounter.

While the latter scenario is obviously the better choice, achieving this level of preparation is no small task. Take time and invest in this aspect of the effort and you should expect at least a 10-fold return. Areas to focus on include aligning with the organization's strategy, assembling the stakeholders, and proactively addressing any risks you can conceive of before they arise.

Linking to Organizational Strategy

As you begin your journey, you will need to establish strong linkages between the work you are leading and your organization's reason for being. As you began doing in Chapter 2, look to the organization's strategic goals, principles, or other high-priority and high-visibility initiatives to guide the "why" of your project. Establishing and articulating this alignment early on will be an important tool for gaining support for digital transformation from leadership, board members, and other key stakeholders.

This search for alignment isn't just window dressing to sell this effort to your stakeholders. The goal is to ensure that the work is contributing to the organization's accelerated progress toward a set of preestablished goals and priorities. After all, why reinvent the wheel when the call to action is right there with the leadership's seal of approval? Establishing this alignment early on, before you communicate the need for digital transformation more broadly, will also lessen the chance that the effort is perceived as a solution in search of a problem.

Once this alignment is established and as you begin to socialize the idea of digital transformation within your organization, you'll want to clearly communicate the "why" using language that reflects a thorough understanding of your organization's strategy, purpose, and culture. This is the time to lay the groundwork before you begin diving into the specifics of the exact changes to be implemented. What better way to start the transformation journey than with strong backing from all who are already 100% bought in to the organization's vision and purpose?

Identifying Key Stakeholders

Digital transformation is largely a matter of mobilizing the right people at the right time, around a shared set of goals and desired outcomes. But where to begin?

At this early stage of the digital transformation effort, the goal is to identify key stakeholders, those who will significantly influence, guide, or impact the success of the project, or, thought of in another way, anyone who could prevent or significantly slow down the achievement of your goals and objectives if they are not fully on board from the early stages of the project.

So how do you identify these influential leaders and coworkers at your organization? First, brainstorm a list of natural allies who support technology and innovation or whose opinion carries a lot of weight. Then consider people who may be critical or suspicious of (or oblivious to) the project who fit the definition of key stakeholder. You'll need to bring them on as supporters as well.

Key stakeholders include staff members, partners, beneficiaries, or other influencers who have an important role to play in the digital transformation effort. As you progress in your digital transformation journey, you will have the opportunity to engage with many stakeholders and hear from them firsthand about their needs and expectations in relation to this project.

With these people in mind, see the next section, "How to Build a Key Stakeholder Map," for a method you can use to profile each individual in terms of their motivations and concerns, as well as their interest in and potential impact on your project. This information should be kept confidential, since its purpose is to guide you and your closest collaborators in tailoring messages and strategies designed to get this important group of people to stay supportive and engaged throughout the digital transformation journey.

Stakeholder mapping is a foundational step for any change initiative. You will need the support and involvement of many influential people within your organization, in leadership and elsewhere, to move the digital transformation effort forward. And if they don't already see the importance and value to the organization of what you're trying to do, now is the time to convince them.

How to Build a Key Stakeholder Map

A stakeholder map consists of the landscape of key leaders and other influencers in all affected parts of your organization that will be pivotal to the success of the digital transformation project. Put on your anthropologist hat and set aside any preformed opinions or biases you may have from working with these people in the past. Objectively examine and try to define their values, goals, and concerns. And because we bring our personalities to work with us, think about how each person's personality factors into their orientation toward the project and how they might respond, positively or negatively, to the different tactics you will use to get or keep them on your side.

Once you've completed this initial mapping step, you'll have a clear view of where more work is needed to assemble your dream team of project allies. With this team in place, you'll be primed to make a strong case for change with these people standing firmly by your side.

(Continued)

(Continued)

It may take time, and some intelligence gathering from others in the know, to complete this exercise. This is time well spent, because getting the right people in your court at this stage will make for smooth sailing at later stages of the journey.

The following is a suggested format for gathering the right information. Feel free to modify based on what makes sense for your organization.

First, gather the basics:

- Name
- Title
- Years at organization

Then go into their specific relationship to the digital transformation effort:

- **Relationship to the project:** If they have a formal relationship to the effort, such as executive sponsor, list it here; otherwise, put "none."
- **Decision authority:** Does this person have budget, strategy, or other levels of authority over the project?
- **Influenced by:** Who has major influence over this person? Think about those who you may need to work with to persuade this person to change their thinking.
- **Has influence over:** Whom does this person influence? Think in terms of what people may be swayed in a negative direction if this person is not fully supportive of the project.
- **Level of influence:** What is this person's overall level of influence in relation to the project, regardless of their formal role or decision authority?
- **Project sentiment:** What is their current level of support for the project? This will come in handy as you review this worksheet to determine where you should apply efforts to build more support.

- **Areas of interest:** Gather whatever intelligence you can about what is most interesting and important to this person in organizational terms. Are they focused on technology advancement, organizational performance, employee engagement? Be as specific as you can so this information can be used to guide how and when you communicate with this person.
- **Values:** While a little squishier, values can reflect what is underneath this person's work behaviors and decisions. Do they value human interaction over technological efficiency? Are they a champion of equity and inclusion? Values could also include work performance-related motivators, such as the need to hit certain targets or KPIs, being in line for a promotion, or plans to retire next year.
- **Hopes/aspirations:** This one may require some actual conversations with the person in question. You'll want to capture what their vision is for how this effort could positively impact the organization, even in vague terms. Where possible, be sure to document where this vision aligns or merges with other organizational priorities on their radar.
- **Fears/concerns:** Again, actual conversations are best to gather this information but you may already be well aware of the fears or concerns this person has in relation to the digital transformation effort. If you're not comfortable asking about this at an early stage of the project, take your best guess. Chances are you're mostly right!
- **Engagement tactics:** Think about the best way to keep this person engaged in the effort over the long term. This may involve bringing in some of their direct reports during critical project milestones or providing the person with regular updates. Make sure to think about your engagement tactics from their point of view, not just what would be most convenient or logical from your perspective.

(Continued)

(Continued)

Once you have this information mapped out, it might be a good idea to review with your closest project collaborators and discuss tactics for moving forward. For people who have a more negative project sentiment, you'll want to have an engagement approach specifically tailored to moving them up the ladder. Remember that not everyone will become a major supporter, and it might not be worth the effort to get them, even if it were possible. Focus on building more support among those who are already somewhat supportive, while moving those in the negative column to at least a more neutral sentiment so they don't stand in the way of progress.

Prepare to spend significant time on the soft skill of stakeholder engagement. There is considerable "shadow work" involved with maintaining your relationships and connection with key stakeholders. This can look like a coffee date, quick one-on-one, email updates, or stopping by someone's office. Your outreach can go a long way in making people feel included and invested in the digital transformation, especially those who have the sway or authority to make or break the project.

Forming the Project Team

The success of the project will largely be determined by having the right people involved throughout the process. Three groups are needed for a well-executed digital transformation project: the core project team, a steering group, and champions. I'll discuss each in the sections that follow.

CORE PROJECT TEAM

The core project team is responsible for performing and coordinating the tactical, day-to-day project activities. If you are in a position to choose the members of the digital transformation project team, choose carefully. This will be the group of people who stay with the project from start to finish, living the inevitable ups and downs that every complex project produces. Look for people who possess resilience, integrity, skill, loyalty to the cause, unwavering enthusiasm, and, of course, adequate time and energy to see things through. You may find that many people express interest in being a part of the effort but lack one or more of these qualities. If you are the person assembling this team, this is where discernment will be needed to select only those who can truly rise to the occasion.

At a basic level, the project team should be composed of an executive sponsor, a capable project manager, and subject-matter experts having knowledge and skills critical to the project's successful completion. If all or most of the real work will be led internally rather than with the help of consultants, the team should be composed primarily of "doers," people who will be hands-on throughout the project and have dedicated time to devote to it. For those who don't fit this description, consider inviting them to serve as a steering committee member or advisor, or a champions group member (see the section "Recruiting Champions" later in this chapter for more on this). Although the composition of the core team may evolve based on the stage of the project, certain members, including the project manager and representatives from key departments, should be consistent throughout.

Think back to the reflection on your leadership skills and style that you did at the end of the previous chapter. Review your strengths and areas for growth as a leader and let this also guide your selection of project collaborators. What are the skills, personalities, and positions that will take your project to the finish line and bolster your own skills where needed? There's a long road ahead, so also consider who you'll enjoy working with. Never underestimate the importance of chemistry, compatibility, and fun when it comes to a good team.

Among the people you have spoken with about this effort so far, it's likely that some individuals stood out as potential project team members. Maybe they were really fired up about the prospect of digital transformation. Maybe they are a critical strategic partner because they run a department that will be deeply affected by the coming changes. Or perhaps they are someone who could be an obstacle to progress if you don't include them in a meaningful way. Check out the next section, "How to Assemble the Right Project Team," for more on getting the right mix.

How to Assemble the Right Project Team

Leading a digital transformation project that will likely impact the day-to-day work of many or all employees takes more than just a single individual or department to lead such an effort. You need an enthusiastic, powerful, and diverse project team to successfully deliver on the project objectives. As you recruit your dream team, consider the key positions to fill, and necessary technical and interpersonal skills to include.

Key Project Roles

Executive sponsor: This business leader, ideally a member of the executive team, is responsible for securing and maintaining executive buy-in, making high-level decisions about the scope, and approving the budget. They must be sufficiently engaged in the project and have some skin in the game to be effective.

Project manager: This mid- or top-level manager oversees the actual implementation of the digital transformation project. They are responsible for calling the plays, such as setting the project management approach, maintaining the workplan, and keeping the project on time, in scope, and within budget. They need enough technology knowledge to communicate effectively with department leads and external resources, but interpersonal skills are the most important quality. Throughout the project, they will have to negotiate, resolve staff conflicts, and manage risk.

IT experts: You will definitely need IT expertise on your project team. While some responsibilities might be outsourced to external resources, you must include internal IT staff who understand your current systems, will oversee any backend integration, and will manage and maintain the new systems moving forward.

Team members: The rest of your project team is made up of a diverse group of interested and invested key staff. These members will provide input on the specific aspects of the project, from who should be consulted at different stages to what digital tools and approaches will meet staff requirements. The exact number and makeup should be tailored to your specific project. For an enterprise-wide solution, perhaps one representative per major department is sufficient.

Preferred skills: Knowledge of how technology functions within the organization, and where there are unmet needs, is necessary for at least some members of the project team. Where members aren't tech savvy, they should possess a deep understanding of the business needs the project will address. In addition to these areas of knowledge, consider recruiting individuals with the following skills and experience:

- ◆ Complex project planning and execution
- ◆ Organizational strategy
- ◆ IT governance
- ◆ Internal communications
- ◆ Creative problem solving
- ◆ Relationship management and consensus building

Other Considerations

Not every organization will have a deep roster to choose from, so you might need to be creative as you recruit your team. Other factors to consider:

Availability: Project teams require a significant time commitment, so look for colleagues who can contribute consistently, even if they might not be your natural top choice.

Experience: Some of the highest-performing team members might be rookies, with little experience or tenure in the company. Benefit from their unique perspective and fresh energy and mentor or develop other skills as needed.

Loyalty to project goals: Someone who is passionate about the initiative but lacks some of the other desired knowledge and expertise might be willing to contribute to the project in unexpected ways. Don't overlook their potential value.

Once you have shortlisted the people you'd like to include, you may want to run it by colleagues and other trusted collaborators to get some additional perspective. Then you'll want to prepare a well-thought-out project charter (see "Digital Transformation Project Charter Outline") to help you communicate the goals, expectations, time commitments, and benefits of the project to your prospective team members so they know what they're signing up for.

Finally, when your team is assembled, it's time to plan your project kickoff meeting. And because it's never too late to become a better meeting facilitator, see "How to Run Great Meetings" at the end of this chapter for some valuable tips and tricks.

Digital Transformation Project Charter Outline

Use this template to create a concise project charter that you can use to recruit and align members of the digital transformation project team.

Project Name

Project Start and End Dates

Charter Last Updated

Purpose

Clearly state the overarching purpose of the project in one to three sentences.

Objectives

List the specific objectives that the project will seek to achieve

People

First list the core team members, including their formal work titles, as well as their role on this project (e.g. executive sponsor, project manager, etc.).

If you are engaging consultants to support the project, list them in a separate section with their designated roles.

Finally, list any key stakeholders with job titles and, if relevant, their specific relation to the project.

Potential Risks/Barriers to the Project

Content for this section should be generated through a thought exercise involving all project team members. It's a great first order of business for the project kickoff meeting. During this discussion, try to list all factors, inevitable or not, in or out of the project team's control, that may place the project's success at risk. Some common factors include:

- Change fatigue
- Competing organizational initiatives
- Lack of buy-in
- Limited employee understanding of anticipated benefits

Once these risks are articulated, you will want to come back to them as you develop a change management plan at later stages of the project.

Project Management

Things to list here include:

- Where project files will be stored
- Where the project work plan will be maintained
- Where communication will take place outside of meetings (collaboration tool, email, etc.)
- Frequency of regular meetings
- Technology used for virtual meetings
- Mandatory versus optional attendees of regular meetings

Project Communications

While a more robust approach to change communication will come later, for now focus on groups that need to be regularly informed of the project progress. The table format can be used to gather the necessary details. It is a good idea to include periodic all-staff updates even at this early stage, to build interest and support for the work to come.

(Continued)

(Continued)

Who	What	When	Responsible	Purpose
Core project team	Status meeting	Weekly	[Person responsible for organizing the meeting]	Review progress Discuss issues and needs Plan activities
Senior leadership team	Project update email	Monthly	[Person responsible]	Update on progress Raise issues/concerns/ needed decisions
All staff	Project update at All Staff Town Hall	Bi-Monthly	[Person responsible]	Highlight progress and what to expect Share opportunities for involvement

Assembling a Steering Group

The steering group, a strategically minded team, is a highly valuable addition to your project pantheon. While there may be cases where it's simply impossible to pull such a group together, it is certainly worth advocating for. This group will advise on and possibly engage in decision-making around the key aspects of digital transformation effort while lending their support to overcome obstacles along the way.

Steering group members should be senior staff (not necessarily C-suite but certainly decision-makers) representing all key business functions that will have a stake in or be significantly affected by the outcomes of the digital transformation project. Since these folks generally have very limited time and mental bandwidth for new projects, it might require some effort to "sell" the idea to your potential recruits. One way to do this is to develop a draft steering group charter, which lays out the purpose of this group, time requirements, type of input that will be needed, and more, to clarify and validate with others what the roles of this group could or should be. Importantly, this charter should be revisited by the actual group members once they're on board so that they can fully own the form and function of the group. You can use the steering group charter template provided to develop a plan for how this group will run and share it with prospective members.

Before going off and starting a new group, think about whether a group already exists that comprises the right, or almost right, mix of people. If your organization is already overloaded with steering groups, you'll want to make sure that a new group is called for, as it may be easier, faster, and more accepted to repurpose an existing one.

A well-functioning steering group will support the widespread adoption of the upcoming changes and will likely play a key role in planning, budgeting, and prioritizing digital transformation activities now and into the future. It should be approached as a group that will exist in perpetuity, or at least until the digital transformation effort has reached a mature and stable state. This group can also be responsible for reviewing or revising relevant policies, making decisions around departmental budgets and staff-time allocations, and reviewing meaningful metrics once changes are implemented.

Digital Transformation Project Steering Group Charter Template

This template provides a starting point for the creation of an internal, cross-cutting group of staff to guide and oversee the digital transformation project. If appropriate, this committee may be transitioned into the Digital Workplace Governance Committee at the conclusion of the digital transformation project (see Chapter 12 for more on this).

Group Purpose

The [GROUP NAME] works to ensure that the digital transformation project is aligned with the organization's strategic goals and objectives as well as the objectives and work processes of all key business units. The primary function of the [GROUP NAME] is to provide cross-cutting, executive-level guidance, and oversight of the digital transformation project and related IT and business process decision-making.

(Continued)

(Continued)

Scope

The [GROUP NAME] is an oversight body responsible for maintaining a holistic, contextualized approach to digital transformation while also ensuring continual feedback and knowledge flows leading to greater IT system efficiency and efficacy and related process improvements. The scope of the [GROUP NAME] includes the following:

♦ Ensure the organization's digital transformation strategy is aligned to the organization's strategic objectives (e.g. employee engagement, revenue generation, efficiency, etc.).

♦ Ensure that a holistic digital transformation vision, informed by end user needs, is commonly understood and supported by leadership and communicated widely to staff.

♦ Ensure the digital transformation project is aligned with business priorities and related organizational strategies.

♦ Support the application of IT and digital transformation best practices from our sector and beyond.

Guiding Principles

In carrying out its work, the [GROUP NAME] will adhere to and broadly instill within the organization the following principles:

1. All major IT systems should support equitable access to critical data and information, knowledge exchange, and informed decision-making across the organization.
2. Where possible, systems should be cloud-based to limit the burden on IT resources.
3. System requirements and use cases should be thoroughly scoped and documented *before* system selection and configuration in consultation with representatives from all anticipated user groups.

4. Systems should be user-friendly, supporting use by those with limited IT skills, and allowing for in-house configuration and management.
5. Employees should be well equipped to make best of their digital tools, through a combination of tailored training and support approaches that meet people where they are.
6. Where appropriate, systems should satisfy the needs of employees at every level of the organization
7. New systems should represent an improvement over the systems they are replacing (if any) in one or more of the following ways: (1) simplification of system architecture through reduction of and/or integration with existing systems, (2) cost savings in terms of licensing and/or maintenance, (3) alignment with strategic priorities, and/or (4) ability to address critical gaps in organizational capabilities and business processes.

Membership

The membership of the [GROUP NAME] is aimed at supporting meaningful engagement of representatives from all key departments in coordination and joint decision-making related to the digital transformation project. Current membership is as follows:

Co-chairs: These are the leaders of the group, and can rotate annually if needed.

Facilitators: They are responsible for meeting logistics and communication, including preparation and circulation of agendas and meeting minutes.

Advisors: Subject-matter experts at any professional level can contribute to discussions on an as-needed basis.

Members: Senior staff with budgeting and decision-making authority for their respective departments should represent all key business functions.

(Continued)

(Continued)

Process

Meeting frequency: Meetings will be held once per month, or more frequently as needed. A virtual meeting option will be provided for remote participants.

Meeting agendas: Meeting agendas will be prepared by the facilitators and circulated to all members and invited advisors prior to the meeting. Agenda items for the next meeting will be solicited from participants at each meeting.

Decision-making: In cases where a decision is brought in front of the committee, decisions will be made by a two-thirds majority. A vote must be received from all members in order for the decision to be valid. Members may collectively decide to delay a decision until further information and/or feedback can be solicited from outside the committee.

Routine communication: Facilitators will record meeting minutes for each meeting and share them with all group members. Co-chairs will send communications out to all staff at least quarterly to update the organization on the committee activities and provide a mechanism for employee feedback and questions.

Recruiting Champions

Champions are enthusiastic supporters who can serve as advisors, test users, and ultimately the primary means by which changes will take hold across the organization. Champions are critical to the success of any change effort and do not require a great deal of structure to be effective. For all these reasons, they are considered indispensable to the digital transformation effort.

Champions are typically staff member volunteers from across the organization who are invested in the success of the digital transformation effort and will generate interest and excitement about the effort in their respective teams and peer groups. As an informal extension of the project team, champions serve as user representatives and advocates, providing feedback at critical stages of tool design, implementation, and rollout. Champions also support staff adoption of new tools and behaviors by modeling new ways of working and providing informal user support to their colleagues.

While there is no ideal number of champions, there should be enough people to adequately support your organization's size and represent most user types and groups. This is an area where steering group members can advise on the composition of the group and may also be needed to gain approval for a small allowance of these staff members' time.

When you are ready to recruit champions, you can provide a program description to team leaders and interested individuals to spark interest while clearly laying out what is expected. Use the Champions Program Description template provided as a starting point.

Digital Transformation Champions Program Description

This template provides a description of a champions program designed to provide a way for people from across the organization to play a meaningful role in the digital transformation effort.

Members

Members should represent a cross-section of the organization, primarily at the sub-management level, representing all distinct departments or units. Membership can rotate, but it is suggested that members be active for at least a one-year term.

All members should:

◆ Be passionate about moving the organization forward
◆ Be enthusiastic about trying and learning new technology
◆ Have a desire to help others learn
◆ Be able to devote three to five hours per month to the program

(Continued)

(Continued)

Member Benefits

- Visible recognition at digital transformation meetings and events
- Being seen by their peers as taking a leading role in an exciting new way of working
- Exclusive access to strategies, plans, and new technology before they are introduced more broadly
- Opportunities to test and provide input into technology enhancements or changes

Group Life Span and Meeting Cadence

Ideally, the champions group will exist in perpetuity, because there will always be a need to have an engaged group of stakeholders supporting and feeding into the success of the evolving digital transformation effort. During less active periods, the group could meet less frequently (i.e. quarterly) as opposed to biweekly or monthly during periods of active implementation or rollout of technology.

Regular Activities

- Collect and share their team's perspectives on the digital transformation project and related technology
- Stay informed about the digital transformation project and share updates with their respective teams
- Provide input and feedback at critical stages of tool selection, implementation, and rollout
- Provide feedback and suggestions on new or existing digital workplace governance policies and processes
- Serve as advocates and role models for new ways of working once digital transformation changes are implemented

Assessing Change Readiness

Digital transformation efforts should proceed in full recognition of an organization's historic approach to technology-related decision-making and organizational change management. In many organizations, this history is checkered at best. Most employees with a longer tenure will remember at least one botched technology project, and chances are they have some residual anxiety, or even trauma, related to what they and others experienced.

As a change leader spearheading an effort that may stir up a complex mix of emotions among affected employees, seek to understand the organization's past relationship with change. For example, if your organization has recently completed a successful change initiative, whether technology related or not, chances are people will be more welcoming, and trusting, of the anticipated changes around digital transformation. Compare that to an organization with a long history of failed or particularly stressful change efforts. How you approach and communicate the desired levels of change in these two scenarios will be significantly different.

In addition to examining your organization's orientation toward change by looking into the past, you'll want to consider current or anticipated future conditions that may affect people's attitudes toward significant change. Are there one or more competing change initiatives that will be running in parallel to yours? Are there major changes – new systems, strategies, or initiatives – planned for the next one to two years that the digital transformation project should take into account?

Assessing the complete landscape when it comes to readiness for change at your organization will be essential to finding the right approaches, language, and timing for your change efforts.

The following questions can be used as a tool for you and your project stakeholders to reflect upon your organization's readiness for change and point to needed preemptive actions or interventions to avoid calamity down the road.

CHANGE READINESS ASSESSMENT

Answer each question with one of the following options: strongly agree, agree, neither agree nor disagree, disagree, strongly disagree.

Experience:

♦ Does our organization have a history of successful, large-scale change efforts (technology-related or not) that this effort should seek to replicate?

♦ Does our organization have a history of successful rollout of new technology, leading to rapid adoption of new tools?

Buy-in/Strategic Alignment:

♦ Is there (or do you expect there will be) strong buy-in from the majority of senior leadership for this change?

♦ Is this effort in alignment or not in conflict with other current or near-future organizational priorities or change efforts?

Processes and Resources:

♦ Does our organization have established processes and communication channels for managing large-scale organizational changes?

♦ Does our organization have dedicated resources for organizational change management (i.e. a responsible team or individual[s]) that we can call upon for this effort?

Culture/Staff Impact:

♦ Does our organization place high value on organizational effectiveness, with staff tending to embrace change that supports this/these objective(s)?

♦ Does our culture make it easy for employees to voice concerns about and/or be involved in shaping organizational changes that affect them?

♦ Is or will the urgent need for this change be apparent to most staff (even if they are not yet aware that it is coming)?

♦ Will staff be able to easily envision how they will directly benefit from these changes?

How to Run Great Meetings

Project managers have to lead many types of meetings – from daily standups with the project team and external vendors to monthly presentations to senior leadership. With the proliferation of remote work, how can project managers make the most of these sessions (and avoid video conference fatigue)?

Basic meeting etiquette necessitates starting and ending on time, having an agenda, and sharing notes, but leaders should aim for more than just efficiency. A great meeting should be both productive and engaging. Here are five tips for making the most out of your meetings:

1. **Don't have the meeting.**

   As you consider scheduling a meeting, first ask yourself, "Is this meeting necessary?" With the abundance of real-time collaboration technology, there are more efficient ways to simply share information or provide status updates. Meetings are most valuable when you need to move a team or project forward when the same can't be easily accomplished using other methods. In the absence of a clear purpose, you could be taking up valuable time and energy that could be better spent on completing tasks. Demonstrate that you value everyone's time, and the organization's resources, by holding meetings only when absolutely necessary. In many cases, the best meeting might be no meeting at all.

2. **Be judicious with your, and everyone's, time.**

   As you develop the meeting agenda, determine how long the meeting needs to be. Don't default to 30 minutes or an hour if a 10- or 15-minute huddle will suffice. Parkinson's law famously states, "work expands so as to fill the time available for its completion."[1] If you have a compressed time frame, there will be added pressure to keep the conversation on track and run through the entire agenda. Here are a few suggestions to make the most of your time:

   (Continued)

(Continued)

♦ **Collect and share materials in advance.** If the goal is to collect feedback on a presentation, circulate it in advance and focus on feedback, rather than a run-through, during the meeting. For team check-ins, ask staff to provide status updates in writing the day before, highlighting any items they would like to discuss with the group.

♦ **Select a good day and time.** No one likes Monday morning meetings! And Friday afternoons are a risky bet. Find the most productive time slot based on the rhythms and work styles of the meeting participants.

♦ **Nominate a timekeeper for longer meetings.** With regular time checks, longer meetings that tend to meander can stay on topic.

♦ **Schedule more frequent, shorter meetings.** If your meetings consistently run over or the team loses focus after 45 minutes, consider changing the length and cadence. Perhaps shorter daily or weekly standups would be more effective and not feel as burdensome.

3. **Welcome all voices.**
A well-run meeting will accomplish more than just unidirectional information sharing. The format should encourage interaction and participation. The meeting leader should create a safe, inclusive environment where everyone feels comfortable and empowered to contribute. How can you cultivate a collaborative meeting culture?

♦ **Get to know each other.** Especially for new teams and ad hoc mashups, time spent on icebreakers (I know, but they do work) or small talk is a well-spent few minutes that can go a long way in building trust and raising levels of comfort among even the most introverted among us.

♦ **Use questions to start a dialogue.** Ask "How might we . . ." or "How can we help?" questions to get the ball rolling and throughout the session. Don't save questions for the end or you might hear crickets.

♦ **Encourage everyone to participate.** All meeting participants are there for a reason. If necessary, pose specific questions to those who are quieter to help their voice be heard. But don't push too hard if they truly don't have anything to add. If someone is dominating the conversation, thank them for sharing and ask to hear from others.

♦ **Welcome diversity of thought, and even conflict.** Divergent opinions ward off groupthink. Those who challenge the predominant opinions of the group contribute enormously to the effectiveness of meetings. As a leader, verbally encourage and acknowledge these contributions to promote honesty and creative thinking.

4. **Don't fumble the ball.**
Is there anything more frustrating than having a "productive" meeting that goes nowhere? To ensure you follow through on any commitments or decisions, reserve time at the end of each meeting to decide what the next steps are, who is responsible, and the expected time frame. By asking "who's got the ball?" (or "who will do what by when?"), you can identify clear action items and determine how to follow up.

Meeting notes are a vital tool to document discussions and drive next steps. While they should be shared with all attendees as soon as possible after the meeting, there could be value in sharing with those who weren't invited. Their work may intersect with yours in a way you can't envision, so openness could lead to more collaboration. If side discussions were tabled, include these "parking lot" items in the notes so staff can decide how to handle them offline.

(Continued)

(Continued)

5. Optimize online meetings

Virtual meetings are now the norm but that doesn't mean that awkward and painful moments won't continue. In addition to the tips above, there are a few other things to keep in mind when leading virtual meetings.

♦ **Choose the right mix of technology.** A stripped-down audio or video call may be fine for small groups. Large group discussions and planning sessions may benefit from additional features, such as virtual white-boards, live polls, breakout rooms, and more. Be creative and don't be afraid to test out new methods when things start feeling stale.

♦ **Encourage engagement through active facilitation.** More people will try to multitask from home, so set ground rules and use video when possible. Without in-person social cues, participation might be more uneven, so the meeting lead might need to be more proactive than usual. Cut people off (interrupt if necessary!) or call on people by name (don't just "open the floor") to ensure everyone can be heard.

♦ **Allow for watercooler talk.** While you don't want to waste anyone's time, you need to put more effort into building rapport in an all-virtual environment. Even if it's a group that meets frequently, build in time at the start for small talk or share something humorous to rekindle personal connections as people jump from meeting to meeting.

Meetings are an irreplaceable tool to consult coworkers, solve problems, make decisions, move projects forward, and in the age of largely remote work, build community. But without the right structure or thoughtful facilitation, they can easily become a drain on staff time and an exercise in futility. Clarify the purpose, trim unneeded time, and maximize participation. As a result, your meetings will be productive, engaging, and even enjoyable!

Your Assignment

- Prepare the project team charter using the template provided and recruit project team members who have the desired qualities and available bandwidth.
- Prepare the steering group charter using the template provided and share it for discussion with potential group members.
- Prepare the champions group description, ideally with input and review from project team and steering group members. Once they're in agreement on the nature of the role, it's time to start seeking volunteers from across the organization.
- Using the change readiness assessment, begin to fill in the answers to each question. You can begin practicing your empathy skills here from the previous chapter by providing two sets of answers. First answer from your own perspective, and the answer from the perspective of a staff member at your organization who might have been part of, or affected by, a recent change effort. You may even want to provide multiple sets of answers from different perspectives or personas, such as a champion, naysayer, or other position. If feasible, you may want to gather responses to these questions from your project team, steering committee, and champions. If you do, be sure to reflect and discuss the results together to consider how they should influence the approaches to change you will use for the current project. Take note of where your answers, or those that you guessed for others, differ. What does that tell you about your own projections and perceptions? How will this guide you in your work going forward? Note anything important in

(Continued)

(Continued)

your journal that you may want to come back to at key points along the way.

You can also provide this assessment as a survey for other key people in the organization, such as the leadership team. I have often been surprised at how much disagreement there can be among leaders' responses to these questions, which demonstrates yet another potential challenge the project team should take under consideration.

PART II

Designing the Ideal Digital Workplace

The act of intentionally designing the digital workplace provides opportunities for revisiting past assumptions and reflecting on the goals and desired outcomes of the digital transformation effort. Through this process, you and your collaborators will listen and empathize with the experiences of people across the organization while taking an honest and in-depth look at the current enterprise tech stack.

In addition to articulating the needs and challenges that the digital transformation project will address, you will also have the opportunity to imagine new and innovative approaches that represent a true departure from the status quo. Even if some of these dreams seem out of reach, no idea should be overlooked at the outset. There will be time for editing later. First, draw inspiration from wherever you can find it. Even pie-in-the-sky ideas can spark innovative yet practical solutions. Just because you're mining for gold, don't ignore the diamonds directly in your path!

CHAPTER 5

Looking

W hen I begin working with a new organization, one of the first things I do is review a current inventory of their enterprise technology. As an experienced practitioner, I can often spot potential issues by simply viewing a list of all business applications in use. And in organizations where no such list exists, that is itself an issue!

Be prepared to make some new discoveries as you embark on this path. You and others may be surprised at the sheer number of different systems in use at your organization – both sanctioned and unsanctioned. Shadow IT is called shadow for a reason. You'll have to dig deep and assure the people you are interviewing that they will not be blamed if they disclose their deepest IT secrets.

The systems map and inventory you create in this chapter will highlight the overlaps and redundancies in your current technology stack. It will also uncover the systems that are over- or underutilized and the major opportunities for cost savings and efficiency gains. Presented alongside the findings from your stakeholder discovery activities (see Chapter 6, "Listening"), the information you gather will demonstrate that there is a real cost associated with doing nothing or maintaining the status quo. Get ready for some rich and illuminating discussions!

It might be helpful to imagine our friend Marie Kondo as she gazes into her clients' disheveled closets. She is no doubt recording several key data points, invisible to the casual observer, that will inform her tidying strategy and approach to communicating about the change to her clients. That's the wisdom that comes from years of experience dealing with similar sets of circumstances.

Do not expect the people involved in your digital transformation effort to have Kondo's discerning eye. There will be quite a bit of work to translate what you observe into tactical digital transformation steps and related communication. You and your collaborators will be responsible for this translation before presenting your findings to others in the organization. It can be dangerous to assume that others, presented with the raw facts around the current state of your digital environment, will immediately see the need for change, or understand why one approach makes more sense than another.

In one memorable client engagement, we worked for weeks to uncover the challenges around a particular on-premise financial management system. The system had been customized and modified over the years to such a degree that no one inside or outside the organization understood how to fix or enhance the system to meet the organization's changing needs. Nearly everyone we met with during our discovery process spoke passionately about how difficult the system was to use and how they wanted to see it replaced. Within our project team, which included the business owner of the system, there was consensus that this system "had to go," and as quickly as possible. Based on this, I assumed that recommending the replacement of this system would be well received and not cause any surprises or controversy. I could not have been more wrong!

As I presented our discovery findings and recommendations deck to the leadership team, which included the chief financial officer (CFO), who was the executive sponsor of the digital transformation effort, I saw her eyes grow wide and her face redden as I flipped to the slide on replacing the financial management system. She was irate, questioning the rationale we had put forward, which included quotes from end users and startling stats about how many system-related issues were causing grief for multiple departments. Ultimately, we were pressured to remove the recommendation from our deck, pushing it over to a "considerations for the future" slide and softening the language considerably.

Six months later, well after the completion of our engagement, I received a call from the business owner of the financial management system who had been a member of our project team. The company that produced the software for that system was deprecating it, meaning they would no longer support its use. The organization was now rushing to find a replacement with the CFO's full support. After I allowed myself a moment to gloat, I took a step back. Reflecting on the experience, I felt that I had let the organization down. If I had not wrongly assumed that the CFO would understand what appeared to me and many others as an obvious need, I could have approached the presentation of our recommendations and the conversations leading up to it differently. Maybe I could have brought a more convincing case that addressed the CFOs natural fears and concerns around eliminating a hobbled yet highly critical business system.

The moral of this story is that it is dangerous to assume that every stakeholder will draw the same conclusions from the facts you are sharing. Once again, empathy is your friend in these situations. Had I thought more deeply about some of the resistance the CFO had, I probably would have anticipated that she would feel resistance to such a significant change. A more skillful approach, which can be supported by a thorough stakeholder mapping exercise that we discussed earlier, can make all the difference when supporting an organization to move away from problematic, but deeply entrenched key systems.

For those who are relatively new to digital transformation or who do not consider themselves technology experts, doing a deep dive into your organization's technology stack and drawing conclusions about what should be done can be intimidating and fraught with potential landmines like the one I described. But there's nothing to fear. Start by simply listing every business application in use and then categorizing it according to its purpose. A picture will start to emerge and messages can be carefully crafted after the project team does its discovery work. Later in this chapter we'll guide you on creating a literal picture, or map, to make it easier for you and others to understand the current state of the digital workplace from the point of view of an employee or system owner. Then we'll discuss the art of crafting the right communication. All of these pieces should be used together to provide a rich platform for discussions and reaching consensus on what changes are needed.

And while this chapter comes before the one on listening, you'll find that these activities are closely intertwined. The full meaning, purpose, history, and possible future of each tool you inventory will only become completely clear once you begin listening to the people who use it.

Building an IT Systems Inventory and Map

The act of creating an enterprise IT inventory starts out as a relatively straightforward exercise. If you are in IT, look at the tools that are licensed and/or maintained by your department. If you are outside IT, you can consult with someone in IT who has access to this information. But this is often just the beginning. As I've mentioned previously, these days it's common for there to be significant numbers of applications licensed and managed outside of IT, often without the knowledge or oversight of IT. To get the full picture of what's going on beneath the surface, you will need to survey the full landscape of your digital environment.

One way to obtain a more complete view of systems is to gather this information during your discovery or "listening" activities, which is covered in the next chapter. You may develop an initial list and then continue to add to it as you speak with staff and leaders from across the organization. If you'd rather complete everything at once, you could try meeting with people from each department who might be knowledgeable about the tools that are in use. If this is unrealistic, consider using a staff survey to help capture the needed information (see Appendix B for a sample survey).

At the completion of this exercise, the goal is to have a detailed list of all enterprise technology that contains key pieces of information about each system (see Figure 5.1). If you are looking holistically across the organization – especially in the case of smaller organizations – then your review may encompass most or all IT systems in use. If you are narrowing your focus to one or more business processes or areas of operation, then you'll want to limit your review to all systems related to that process or area, and other systems they connect or integrate with. Be careful not to isolate your view to only those systems directly involved. Remember to think about the relationship between systems that sit in or outside of a given process or set of activities and how a person might interact with them as part of their workday. You may be surprised to find that they are more related than you originally thought!

You'll also want to gather as much information as you can around system costs. Determining costs related to IT system licensing and ongoing maintenance is generally a challenge because many costs can be buried in departmental budgets outside of IT. Even when systems are paid for out of the IT budget, other departments may foot the cost of system maintenance or upgrades. In my experience, trying to get an entirely accurate picture of overall IT system spend can become a dizzying and often soul-crushing experience that can significantly slow the project's momentum.

With this in mind, try to uncover as much cost data as you can while expecting it will remain somewhat incomplete for the time being. Any potential savings you can demonstrate, for instance, by eliminating redundant systems, will help build a stronger case for the digital transformation project in these early stages. Calculating the actual anticipated return on investment (ROI) may be out of reach now but will become easier once the details of the changes to be made have been fully worked out. This buys you some time to keep hammering away at a clear picture of your organization's true IT systems spend, which will likely be far larger than anyone imagined!

Elements of an IT Systems Inventory

Your IT systems inventory should be recorded using a spreadsheet or similar application so that it can be easily digested and modified as the project continues. Suggested columns include the following:

◆ System name
◆ Application or software (if different from system name)
◆ Business owner(s) (typically non-IT staff who are the lead system owners)
◆ Executive sponsor(s) (the person responsible for making budget and other strategic decisions related to the system)

(Continued)

(Continued)

♦ Category (choices can include "communication," "content and collaboration," "data analysis and management," "security," and possibly other categories relevant to your analysis; more about this later in the chapter)

♦ Business process(es) supported (which business processes, if any, the system is related to)

♦ Primary use description (one or two sentences describing how users typically interact with the system, including any key inputs or outputs it relates to)

♦ User group(s) (which teams or departments use the system)

♦ Admin or support staff (people who regularly manage the system or support end users)

♦ Annual licensing cost (per user if SaaS application)

♦ Other notable recurring costs (maintenance, consulting, hosting, upgrades, etc.)

♦ Sanctioned/unsanctioned (note whether the system is considered an official, sanctioned tool or is part of the collection of shadow IT solutions)

♦ System notes (additional information such as whether a system will soon be decommissioned or upgraded, etc.)

Making Sense of the Digital Workplace

Once you have a list of all or most of the enterprise technology in use, along with at least some of the accompanying fields listed in the IT systems inventory, you can begin slotting each tool into its related category. I like to start by looking at the digital workplace from the point of view of the employee or end user, as a collection of tools falling into four basic categories:

Communication: Tools that help people connect and communicate. These include email and email groups (i.e. listservs and distribution groups), chat or instant messaging, discussion boards, and internal communications platforms, including intranets and organizational news platforms.

Content and Collaboration: Tools that help people create, organize, store, and find content. These include tools people use to create documents, file repositories where content is organized and saved, search and filtering tools for finding content, and other content platforms such as wikis or knowledge bases. Intranets may also fit here if they are used to house content beyond that used for internal communications. (It's okay for a system to be assigned to more than one category where this makes sense.)

Data Analysis and Management: Tools that help people store, access, and manage data, and transform it into useful information. These include all kinds of databases, including CRMs and financial management systems, spreadsheet-based trackers, and analysis tools, as well as data visualization and dashboard creation tools. Also included are tools for consolidating and analyzing data from multiple sources, including data "lakes" or data warehouses.

Security: Tools that help maintain the security of the digital workplace. These include user authentication and identify manage tools like single sign-on (SSO), external threat protection for spam, phishing, and the like, and device management, as well as insider risk management tools that prevent unsafe practices by staff.

Increasingly, many of the enterprise IT tools you list may have one or more features enhanced by artificial intelligence (AI), machine learning (ML), and/or process automation. If you feel these capabilities are significant and distinct enough to deserve one or more separate categories, then go ahead and add them. There is no right or wrong when it comes to the exact number or type of categories you use, only that the categories represent meaningful "buckets" of functionality for how your organization works and thinks about its tech stack. If you want to simply note that these enhanced features are present, consider adding one or more columns to note these capabilities so they are not forgotten.

While the act of slotting digital tools into a handful of broad categories may seem overly simplistic, I am continually amazed at the power of this framework for making sense out of the most chaotic digital environments. As you will see later in this chapter, using these categories to visually map each tool goes even further to help us understand the exact nature of the chaos we are seeking to unravel.

Once you have assigned each piece of technology to its proper category, opportunities for reducing duplication, establishing needed linkages and integrations, and automating related business processes will begin to crystalize before your eyes. This is where the magic of intentionally designing the digital workplace begins to happen.

But first, let us take a deeper look at each category.

COMMUNICATION

Digital tools for communication provide virtual spaces for people to work, learn, and share with one another in a variety of forms. Email is still playing a central role, but with so many was to communicate it is now possible to reduce email volume while providing a better experience around the real-time discussions that help get work done while supporting more meaningful human connections (emojis and GIFs for a start!). In the age of hybrid and remote work, this category is taking center stage, since these tools are the digital fabric that connects employees across the virtual enterprise. Prior to this shift, it was often a collection of haphazardly selected apps suffering from poor adoption and disconnection from the remainder of the digital workplace. That is no longer – or *should* no longer – be the case.

The recipe for success in this category or layer of the digital workplace is simplicity. People must, with absolute clarity, understand where and how to engage with one another in their virtual spaces. Fractured communication with same or similar groups of people across multiple systems is disruptive to work getting done and gives rise to feelings of chaos, disorganization, and disconnection.

Getting it right requires gaining a thorough understanding of the specific flavors of communication taking place in your organization (more on that later) and then designing a configuration of tools that support every **business use case**[1] with little ambiguity around what happens where.

Typical business use cases supported by tools in this category include:

♦ Staff need a central place they can go to catch up on organizational news, access key resources, and feel part of the company culture.

- Department members need to engage in many-to-many discussions with their colleagues in a way that supports instant updates and targeted notifications.
- People across the organization need the ability to send private one-to-one and group chats on an ad hoc basis.
- Organizational leaders need the ability to post news and announcements to all staff, or subsets thereof, that trigger alerts and reminders prompting people to read them.
- Staff need to be able to communicate with people outside the organization in line with the organization's security and compliance policies.

CONTENT AND COLLABORATION

The content management layer contains the systems that support people to organize, store, and find content. Before the advent of cloud-based content management solutions, files primarily resided in locally hosted or on-premise ("on-prem" for short) file servers. While many organizations have fully embraced the cloud, others are maintaining what is referred to as a hybrid environment, with some files stored and managed in on-prem systems, while others are in cloud-based repositories.

The chief complaint people have around tools in this category is that they cannot easily find what they are looking for. One recent poll among knowledge workers found that employees spend roughly two hours per day, or 25% of their work week, looking for documents, information, or people they need to get their work done.[2] A variety of factors contribute to this challenge, some human generated and some more technology driven. When it comes to human factors, people are naturally prone to behaviors that make finding content more difficult – for example, filenames that do not reflect the actual content of the file, and hard-to-navigate and decipher filing structures that make it difficult or impossible for someone to happen upon what they are looking for by simply browsing through.

But there's more to the story. With the arrival of cloud-based file management solutions, search capabilities have advanced significantly. Full indexing of a file's content has made file naming less of a concern, and intelligent search algorithms can serve up more relevant, personalized results based on a file's properties or metadata that indicate when you last viewed it, who created it, and so on.

With the arrival of AI and ML capabilities in off-the-shelf content management solutions, the ability to find content quickly and easily will continue to advance rapidly.

But how to deliver on the goal of easy search and discovery? This can be a significant challenge in environments containing terabytes of data stored across multiple systems, each with its own filing and retrieval norms. The best place to start, similar to the Communication layer, is by designing an approach that requires the least number of systems or "places" a person must use to store and retrieve files. In the era of cloud file management solutions, this can often mean migrating from several disconnected platforms to one or a few central platforms divvied up into meaningful content "neighborhoods" or partitions. This allows people to master the art of organizing, searching, and browsing using one set of tools, while still being able to zoom in or out of different areas with ease.

Centralized file management also supports a greatly enhanced search experience, where people can choose to conduct *global* or *local* content searches from one location without the need for more sophisticated enterprise search[3] capabilities. It can also lead to better adoption of enhanced content management features, such as managed metadata, filtering, and more. Again, the key here is to incentivize people to master one set of features and functionality and use them to their highest degree.

Content collaboration is another often cited pain point in this category of tools. In some cases, people can easily work with people within their department by co-editing and commenting on files but find it difficult to work across departments or divisions due to intentional or accidental information silos and security constraints. In other cases, internal collaboration is well supported but working efficiently with people outside the organization is challenging. These difficulties can lead staff to employ workarounds, including the use of unsanctioned tools. Aside from cluttering an already crowded digital workplace, use of unsanctioned tools can lead to content sprawl, loss of valuable content resulting from turnover, and increased security risks.

Be sure to investigate and document all of the different flavors or of content and collaboration prevalent at your organization. Later you will explore how digital tools can support the most efficient and secure workflows in each case, minus the workarounds.

Typical business use cases supported by tools in this category include:

- Departments need to store and collaborate on files that only they can access.
- Staff can search for files using a natural language search and can use filters to quickly narrow the results.
- Content managers can apply metadata and/or tags to files or collections of files to control how they show up in search results, and to allow for more granular filtering and sorting.
- Staff can easily collaborate on and share files within and outside their departments.
- Staff can easily collaborate on and share files with people outside the organization while complying with organizational security and compliance requirements.

DATA ANALYSIS AND MANAGEMENT

This category includes applications that store, retrieve, query, or analyze data. In an ideal digital workplace, this layer consists of one or more systems serving as the source of truth for all business-critical data. These tools also produce analytics and data visualizations, actionable business intelligence, to support data-driven decision-making at all levels of the organization.

It is generally expected that organizational leaders should receive regular helpings of organizational data, often served up on a virtual silver platter of attractive data visualizations. These lovely data products are often painstakingly produced by hardworking analysts and others, out of view from the recipient who remains oblivious to the level of work involved. While these products carry the illusion of certainly with their carefully constructed and notated charts and graphs, the reality is often dramatically different. In conversations with staff involved in the production of data or business intelligence products for their organizations, many have candidly shared their fears and concerns around the accuracy of the underlying data.

This is an open secret in the world of business intelligence and data analytics, so much so that there are numerous jokes, cartoons, and the like reflecting this reality. But the consequences of using inaccurate data for decision-making are no laughing matter. From sleepless nights for data analysts to faulty decisions based on the "numbers," the repercussions are many.

Enter the concept of data democratization. In well-designed data analysis and management layers, data transparency and accountability are baked in. Of course, transparency here means that people who can and should have access to the data do, without difficulty, at all levels of the organization. The more visibility, the more people will naturally discover problems, and the more responsibility data producers will feel for ensuring the data is of high quality. This also goes for analytics and user-friendly dashboards. When designing these products, all data consumers or audiences should be considered, not just those in leadership positions. For example, there are many roles throughout the organization that could benefit from timely access to actionable data, which can serve as an immediate feedback loop. People should be able to see and take action without the aid of live interpretation or a data science degree.

As in the content and collaboration layer, simplicity is the goal. It is useful to start the process of unraveling the data and information management environment using the process of data mapping (see the next section, "Building an Enterprise Data Map"). This fairly simple exercise involves documenting and categorizing all manner of data routinely collected and stored, while identifying which systems are the definitive source for each category of data. Problems can be identified. For example, it might not be clear which system is the definitive source, or often different departments might consider different systems the definitive source for the same data, even though those systems do not talk to one another.

Typical business use cases supported by tools in this category include:

◆ Designated staff need to create and regularly update business data in a system of record, with varying levels of permissions around record types and categories.
◆ Designated staff need to produce reports from multiple systems and combine them into a series of data visualizations and/or dashboards.

- Designated staff need access to real-time analytics to help them track progress or performance based on key performance indicators (KPIs).

Building an Enterprise Data Map

The goal of building an enterprise data map, or a data map covering one or more key areas of enterprise data, is to gain clarity on what data your organization is storing and using and where there are areas of overlap or redundancy between systems. Using this data, you can begin to make sense of your data environment and engage in evidence-based discussions about what aspects of your data management and use capabilities should be improved.

This is best done in a spreadsheet or similar format so that it can be easily read and updated over time. As you make changes to your data systems, this document can serve as a useful reference to keep track of where you were, and where you are going.

Useful elements of a data map are as follows:

- **Description:** Brief description of the data type in terms that are generally understood in your organization (e.g. "marketing leads")
- **Data Object Type:** What type of data object is this, based on the nomenclature used in the system(s) where the data resides? For example, in CRM systems, individual people records are often referred to as "contacts."
- **System of Record:** This is the data system where this data is considered most accurate and up to date. It is usually the source from which other systems pull data if there are integrations between multiple systems.
- **Other Systems:** List any other systems where this data can be found or queried outside of the system of record.

(Continued)

(Continued)

Optional but useful components of the data map, which you may add initially or down the road, include:

- **Data Source(s):** Data collection processes, systems, or other sources that this data originates from
- **Related Reports and Dashboards:** Any standard organizational reports that rely on this data
- **Business Owner(s):** The teams, departments, or individuals responsible for managing this data and/or the system(s) in which it is housed
- **Business User(s):** The teams, departments, or individuals who primarily use this data to perform their work

Once your data map is mostly complete, you can use it as a reference during discussions with staff that focus on the data layer of the digital workplace (more on that in Chapter 6). You will likely continue to gather additional information as you go and this map will be the best place to put it for easy reference, rather than staying buried in discussion notes.

SECURITY

The security layer is the layer least visible to the organization. It is also the critical foundation of any well-designed digital workplace. While the intricacies of what is required at this layer are beyond the scope of this book, I would like to address where this shows up most often as a digital employee experience issue.

Easy access to systems, and the content that resides within them, is a hugely important digital workplace design principle. The catch is that ease of access is often at direct odds with maintaining a high level of information security. I typically hear two very different versions of the same story when it comes to the security layer of an organization. On the one hand, staff complain that security is so restrictive they "cannot get anything done." They often call out the IT people responsible for enforcing security as if they are overzealous mall security guards on a rampage, out to clamp down on anything resembling productivity just because they feel empowered to do so. On the other hand, IT folks are not sleeping well at night and are feeling perplexed and perhaps a bit deflated. They simply do not understand why staff cannot work within these "reasonable" restrictions when the organization's security is at stake.

How to balance these diametrically opposed but equally valid perspectives? First off, it's important to acknowledge that every organization's risk profile and risk tolerance is different. In highly regulated industries or particularly at-risk organizations, security requirements will take precedence over the need to provide a higher degree of individual freedom and flexibility when it comes to accessing information. That said, there is often a lot that can be done to make access to information more effortless and enjoyable while still living up to the organization's security standards. After all, if staff find that getting their work done is simply too difficult under the current conditions, they will resort to using workarounds, such as the use of unsanctioned or shadow systems, that can compromise even the most buttoned-up security environments.

When attempting to better understand an organization's security philosophy, or set of beliefs that drive decision-making in this area, I like to start off with a simple question:

> "In this organization, what would you say is your default approach to information access for staff? Is access generally open unless content needs to be protected? Or is access typically granted based on explicit need?"

It's always surprising to me how this question can give rise to important, in-depth discussions around the philosophical underpinnings of the organization's security approaches. What I have noticed over the years is that the "old" way, before the move to the cloud, was to have information locked down by default. Staff would gain access to information either by belonging to a specific group that had been granted access or by explicitly requesting access. In the latter case, this request was often made not to the content owner or manager, but to IT, since the content owner did not have the ability to grant someone access to the files under their control. This created IT bottlenecks, where people would angrily wait for days for IT to grant them access to the doc they needed to get their work done. In some cases it also led to security risks, where the content owner could not actually "see" who had access to what was under their ownership, nor could they easily undertake a review and correction of permissions around content under their care.

Additionally, the nature of permissions, which were often assigned at the container (i.e. file server or folder) level, made it very difficult to provide more granular, nuanced types of access. For example, if you wanted to give a person access to one document within a secure repository to which they did not have access, the easiest way would be to email a copy. But then what if they needed access to one folder within that repository? And what if they also needed to be able to search within a folder, but only content they had access to? Things can get complicated really fast.

Once cloud file management came on the scene, permissions management could become decentralized, with content owners taking on more control. With this new power came new responsibilities, but employees were often finding themselves poorly prepared to wield such responsibility, if they were even aware they had it. This trend gave rise to new and in some cases increased risks and fears among content owners and IT staff alike. With content easier to find via cloud search, one permission slipup could lead to disastrous consequences. While some rejoiced that silos were breaking down, others were shaking in their boots.

What, then, is the best approach or philosophy when it comes to balancing the need for security with easy access to information people need to get their work done? Not surprisingly, it begins with clearly defining the organization's security and compliance needs. Next, understand where and how employees are experiencing the greatest obstacles and what they are willing, and not willing, to do to make things work better for them and the organization.

I'm struck by how often organizations struggle to articulate the reasons behind their security tools configuration, as if it just appeared one day and everyone agreed and moved on to the next thing. Some you encounter will consider security sacred ground, not to be messed with as part of a human-centered digital transformation process. I urge you to push past this faulty perception. Unless you can address this "last mile" problem by finding a middle way between the impenetrable security fortress and clandestine anarchy, your efforts will not deliver the desired level of positive transformation that employees are hoping for.

Put simply, the security layer, just like every other layer of the digital workplace, must be intentionally designed.

Typical business use cases supported by tools in this category include:

♦ Staff can log in once (i.e. using single sign-on, or SSO) to gain secure access to all key business systems.

♦ Staff can easily and quickly gain access to information they need to perform their work without having to submit a request to IT.

♦ Content owners have visibility into who has access to their content and can control and limit access at the individual file and container levels.

♦ Security levels can be applied selectively to files and folders based on location, information type, actual content, or other variables that will restrict sharing and access to files across different platforms.

Creating a Visual Systems Map

Once you compile the system inventory, I highly recommend you produce an accompanying current-state visual systems map (Figure 5.1). This map is a visual representation of the inventory, less most of the related system details, that can be used to effectively tell the story of the current state of the digital workplace, especially to those who are less familiar with IT or simply more visual in how they take in information.

When you begin to envision the future, this map can be used to guide some of these discussions. One of the key early outputs of the envisioning work covered in Chapter 7 is a future-state version of this map, which will elegantly tell a story of the before and after of the digital transformation effort.

A visual systems map is a visual representation of the IT systems inventory that can help communicate the state of the digital

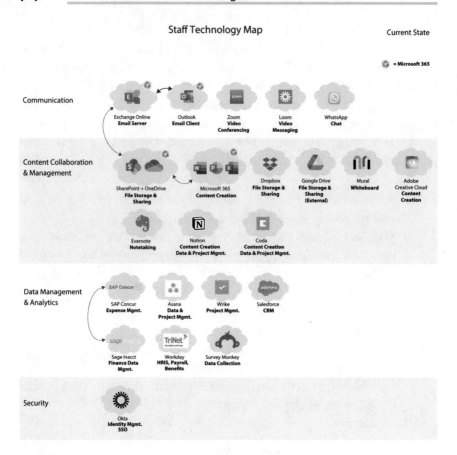

Figure 5.1 Sample visual systems map.

workplace to a broad audience. It is also a useful tool for rich discussion and decision-making around needed system changes.

Use the systems map to:

◆ See all technology at-a-glance
◆ Quickly spot duplication and areas for greater efficiency
◆ Validate the systems inventory and highlight "missing" systems or other incomplete information
◆ Visually represent the chaos and clutter that many are experiencing but do not know how to articulate
◆ Build alternate visual "prototypes" of the future state to consider and share options with stakeholders

The act of creating a visual systems map is a relatively straight-forward exercise that should take minimal effort and time. I like to use a virtual whiteboarding tool for these, but any tool you are most comfortable with will do.

You'll want to organize the map into "layers" representing the different categories of tools we discussed in this chapter, along with any other specialty areas you might be using. I recommend you put these layers in the following order, starting at the top of the map: Communication, Content and Collaboration, Data Analysis and Management, Security.

For each system you place on the map, include the following:

◆ **Icon or logo:** Use whichever best represents the application or platform. (Logos also make it more visually appealing!)

◆ **System name:** This should be the name the system is commonly known under.

◆ **System purpose or function(s):** Briefly state what it does (payroll, expense tracking, etc.).

◆ **Symbols or color coding:** This can be used to show a variety of distinct features. I always use a symbol and/or color to clearly identify shadow/unsanctioned systems.

◆ **Integrations:** Use lines with arrows showing directional data flows between systems that are integrated with one another.

Things to keep in mind when creating a visual systems map:

◆ **Include "shadow" systems in use.** Even though they are unofficial, including these systems in your map will help people grasp the extent of the organization's shadow IT "problem." Some of these shadow systems will surface during the discovery process. Others will come to light in the process of showing this map to others. I recommend using a specific symbol or color to easily identify shadow systems and visually distinguish them from official tools.

◆ **Make it easy to understand and visually appealing.** Use simple visuals (i.e. icons, basic shapes, lines) and a limited color palette, and provide a symbol key to ensure that the map is easily readable. Go for clarity over completeness when it comes to depicting the details of each system. Your inventory can be used as an accompanying document to provide a greater level of detail. Before finalizing the map, show it to people outside of IT to see if it makes sense to them. And keep the design and color palette on brand to reinforce it as a key organizational asset. The goal is to create a visual representation of the state of enterprise technology that any layperson can understand, not a detailed technical diagram.

- **Validate.** Once all systems are logged and organized, confirm the map is accurate before sharing it widely. Find those you trust and walk them through the map to fill in any missing systems or details.

- **Keep the map up to date.** As the digital transformation effort progresses, reflect changes in updates to the map. Consider revisiting and revalidating the map at least once a year (or more, as you make significant updates). Not only will this help identify additional areas for improvement, but it will serve as a record of changes and enhancements over time. The visual systems map is a useful artifact for illustrating progress, showing ROI, and having a foundation on which to build future transformation efforts.

Your Assignment

- Now it's time to roll up your sleeves and apply the process described to your own environment. It might take some detective work depending on where you sit within the organization. If you are in IT, you may already be aware of or have at least a partial list of tools in use at your organization. Start with this if it's available but make sure you gather all the suggested info for each tools listed.

    If you cannot gather all the needed info about each tool easily, just note what's missing and move on. Cost information can sometimes be particularly hard to come by and will not play too important a role until you begin designing for the future in Part 3, so do not let it bog you down. Similarly, you may find that there is not a clear business owner for every system. This is telling and will be something you'll want to come back to later when you begin shoring up your organization's approach to digital workplace governance.

◆ Once your inventory is mostly complete, use your diagramming or whiteboarding tool of choice to create a visual systems map of your current digital workplace, or the section thereof that you'll be focusing on for this initiative. Draw connecting arrows between systems that "talk to each other" through an integration or other type of connection. Once you have your map, keep refining it until you feel like it will tell a clear story to techies and non-techies alike.

◆ Finally, once you have completed the inventory and mapping exercises, write down your reflections of this process so far. Some prompts you can use include:

- What were you surprised about?
- What were you confused about or unsure of?
- What, if anything, brought up feelings of frustration or anger, or made you feel overwhelmed?
- Which aspects of the inventory or map jumped out as being either most in need of fixing or not to be messed with?
- How do you expect others – based on role or personas – to react to the inventory and map?
- In a few words, how would you describe the state of the digital workplace based on these depictions?

CHAPTER 6

Listening

Making a strong case for digital transformation is much like telling a good story. Before getting into the action of your story, your audience will need to understand and empathize with the lead characters and the circumstances in which they find themselves. For people to understand the urgency of digital transformation, they'll need to appreciate the struggles staff have with the current systems.

Listening, or as we consultants call it, "discovery," is a research activity that consists of listening to people from across the organization and providing them with an opportunity to outline the specific challenges and unmet needs they are grappling with. In accordance with design thinking, we don't want to dwell on or predefine the problems, but we do need to understand what we are solving for and where maximum impact can be achieved when changes to the digital workplace are implemented.

The methods are simple. Conduct focus groups, one-on-one interviews, and perhaps a survey or two where staff are invited to share their experiences related to the digital workplace. These discussions will illuminate many shared challenges around current technology, while highlighting which specific tools may be at the center of most pain points. Then it will be much easier to understand the systems inventory and visual map in context and add additional details about each system or tool.

You will also likely uncover additional systems that are not yet captured in your systems inventory. This is another important feature of these discovery activities. Rather than retreading known territory, this is your chance to push the envelope a bit. By probing further into respondents' answers, you can uncover important additional details, such as the system they started using last year as a workaround but didn't want IT to know about.

It is important to complete a thorough discovery *well before* making any changes to the digital workplace. I have had many new clients come to me midway through a failed change process, realizing that they acted too soon before fully understanding the nature of the problems to be solved. This can only lead to improperly selected or poorly designed solutions, which, in turn, lead to discouraged or disengaged employees. By taking a step back, even if you feel you understand exactly what needs to happen, you will be doing your organization, and your professional reputation, a great service and avoid the "solution in search of a problem" epidemic plaguing many modern enterprises.

This is also a good time to reflect on the relative maturity of your digital workplace from the perspective of the people who use it. The Digital Workplace Maturity Assessment in Appendix A provides a high-level view of digital workplace strengths, weaknesses, and gaps and can serve as a useful foundation for the deeper investigation you will undertake during this and subsequent chapters.

Keep in mind that these activities involve a relatively quick scan of people's digital transformation needs and wants. You'll have a chance to delve deeper once you begin moving forward with implementing changes to different aspects of the digital employee experience. For now, the focus is on collecting ideas and anecdotes that will help you build a strong case for change and bring home the real-world struggles people are facing. These concrete examples are especially important to communicate to those in leadership and elsewhere who may not be "feeling the pain" as acutely.

As you gather staff perspectives, you will want to record your findings in a way that makes synthesis and analysis as easy as possible. In my consulting practice, we have developed a method for this that works quite well, both for analysis as well as something that can be used as a historical record of the discovery work. The types of information you'll want to capture through your discovery activities include the following:

- **Challenges:** Anything people raise as a barrier to getting work done
- **Opportunities:** Current or anticipated activities and emerging realities that, if capitalized on, could help advance the way work gets done
- **Quotes:** First-person statements (anonymized, of course) that provide powerful and concise testimony and context to the challenges and opportunities cited
- **List of activities and participants:** Each discovery activity you conduct, along with a list of participants, which will be important for future reference and provide a complete list of all people taking part

Once you have completed the discovery activities, you will synthesize your findings into a rich report or presentation that provides a detailed, easily understandable breakdown of the current state of the digital employee experience and the health and maturity of the digital workplace. The picture that emerges should make it clear how shortcomings in your digital workplace design are reducing work efficiency and effectiveness as well as worker happiness, along with high-level recommendations about top priorities and what can be done to address the organization's biggest pain points.

Who to Include

The solutions to your organization's digital woes may seem obvious to you and your collaborators. "A new database could automate these reports and save us time and money!" But for enterprise-wide digital transformation, you'll have to gather more perspectives before arriving at the right solution.

Interview people at all levels: It takes a variety of perspectives to fully capture the current state. When selecting people to take part in discovery activities, it is important to get broad representation of different groups according to several meaningful variables. These can include:

- Department
- Role or cadre
- Geographic location

♦ Seniority

♦ Tenure

Interview enough (but not too much): The number of people will depend on the size and structure of the organization. Think about what a representative sample of staff would consist of. The goal is "saturation," a term from qualitative research that refers to the point in data collection when no new issues or insights are identified, signaling that an adequate sample size has been reached.

There is no hard and fast rule when it comes to the specific percentage of a population that is needed to reach this point, so the designers of the process will have to exercise their best judgment. For example, are all departments, regions, and staff levels represented? Are people with varying degrees of professional experience and tenure at the organization included? If new insights are still being uncovered toward the end of the process, this is a signal that more people or different groups need to be reached before the saturation point is reached.

Discovery Methods

I will briefly discuss the common discovery methods here, with practical tips on things to look out for and how to know when you've done it "right."

METHOD: FOCUS GROUP

Simple but powerful, focus groups are an opportunity to bring groups of people together to uncover their feelings, unmet needs, and concerns around the digital workplace. This semi-structured conversation is usually led by one person, often accompanied by a notetaker, in a way that encourages free-flowing, candid conversation between 5 and 10 individuals (groups can be bigger, but smaller groups often yield richer and more candid discussion).

It's important to recognize the power dynamics of any group that comes together to speak about conditions in the workplace. For instance, it may be best if people perceived to have responsibility or authority for the aspects of IT or the digital workplace being discussed are not present during the conversation. If they are present, participants may hesitate to voice their true feelings, especially if they are mostly critical of the current state. If you have an outside consultant supporting this work, they could play a useful role here as group facilitator. If it will be internally led, consider recruiting someone who will be seen as a trusted peer by those taking part in the group to serve as the facilitator.

And then there are the power and other dynamics within the group itself. If people from a given team or department are prone to groupthink, design mixed groups that contain people with diverse perspectives. One important group is new hires. But these new staff are often reluctant to share negative experiences about their new workplace when more experienced staff are present. And of course, try to avoid the presence of senior staff when more junior staff should feel free to candidly share their views.

The bottom line is, know your people. People who are highly analytical thinkers may need more time or prompting to unravel their thoughts and get to the matter at hand, while people who tend to express themselves more readily and emotionally can derail or dominate the discussion. The facilitator will have to be able to keep the conversation on track while ensuring that people do not feel alienated or stifled.

If the conversations are taking place virtually, it will be more challenging to read people's expressions and body language and intervene when needed. Equally challenging is ensuring people remain attentive while other people are speaking. A large part of the power of a focus group is bringing people together to reflect on and respond to what other people have to say, not just sharing what's in their own minds. Whether virtual or in-person, sharing ground rules at the outset is an essential part of the focus group experience (see the "Sample Interview or Focus Group Discussion Guide" at the end of this chapter). It may seem pedagogical, but reminding people what's expected of them before diving in is always a good idea.

Focus group sessions generally last 60–90 minutes and will be conducted according to a focus group discussion guide prepared in advance (see the template at the end of this chapter). It is important to clearly state up front – preferably in the session invite – the purpose of the focus group and how the information gathered will be used.

METHOD: ONE-ON-ONE INTERVIEWS

One-on-one interviews for this type of project typically take 30 minutes. These interviews are a good alternative to focus groups in cases where a more personalized approach is desirable. This could be due to the seniority of the interviewee, since leaders may prefer to share their views in private, but could also be appropriate in other circumstances, such as when the subject has very strong opinions, a long history working on related initiatives, or views that may be considered controversial or even potentially harmful to themselves or others if shared in a group setting.

It may be useful to have the interviewer be a neutral party or someone in whom the interviewee has a high degree of trust. Questions often follow a similar or identical flow to that of the focus groups, but this format should allow more time to delve into the specifics of each response.

METHOD: SURVEYS

Surveys can be a powerful tool for reaching wider swaths of the organization and ensuring that people have a channel to provide their thinking anonymously. Most organizations I work with report having some degree of survey fatigue. I take this to mean two things. One, there may be simply too many surveys throughout the year. Two, which tends to be more common, is that staff perceive the surveys as a waste of time, regardless of how many there are, because they don't see a meaningful analysis and interpretation of the results and/or they don't see any action taken based on the survey findings.

When surveys are conducted responsibly, they are a great, time-efficient method for information gathering. They are also a great tool for measuring progress over time. For this reason, timing matters. I suggest using a survey at the very outset of the digital transformation effort before any changes have been made but also before any planned changes have been broadly communicated. Even the notion of what may come may bias people's views or make them less likely to suggest changes not in line with what they believe is being planned.

A few things to keep in mind when developing staff surveys:

Keep it short! Try to limit the survey to around 10 questions or something that people could easily complete in five minutes. This will help people provide focused, high-quality answers.

Make space for deeper thinking. For those who have a lot to say, open comment fields are a great way to capture more nuanced perspectives.

Capture meaningful demographics. For a more meaningful analysis, make sure you capture key information about respondents that you can use to slice and dice your results. This will allow you to break down findings by specific groups of staff to see if there are any meaningful differences or clustering of viewpoints. Typical things to capture include department, seniority or level, years at the organization, and geographic location and/or office.

Craft your questions carefully. How you frame questions can have a big influence on how people respond. The science of surveys is far too great a subject for us to tackle here but I recommend using the simplest possible language, avoiding jargon and ambiguous terms. Once the survey is drafted, it's best to run it by several people with different perspectives, and perhaps different cultural, language, or other backgrounds, so you can fine-tune the language accordingly. I prefer questions framed as positive statements, which respondents rate in terms of how much they agree or disagree. For example, state the question as "I find it easy to locate content that I need to perform my work," instead of, "I find it difficult to . . .

Use the right scale. When using statement-style questions where the respondent rates how much they agree or disagree, use a widely accepted Likert scale format. I suggest a five-point scale, which provides enough options to pick up on both strong and ambivalent feelings without getting too granular. For example, a five-point Likert scale for measuring levels of agreement would be these options: strongly agree, agree, neither agree nor disagree, disagree, strongly disagree. I'm often asked how to interpret a response of "neither agree nor disagree." While it takes some reading between the lines, I typically take this response to mean one of the following: (1) the person hasn't thought enough about the issue at hand to have strong feelings about it, (2) the person doesn't fully understand the question, or (3) they truly have mixed feelings.

Analyze, meaningfully. Once the results are in, it will be tempting to interpret them according to your own beliefs and biases. Try to resist that urge. Some results may be very definitive, such as that 80% feel strongly positive or negative about something. But many results can be more nuanced. This is where deeper analysis filtering by the demographic characteristics you collected will be useful. You use filters to compare distinct groups, such as by location, tenure, and so on, to detect distinct trends or differences between them.

Apply knowledge through interpretation. Once you have the basic analysis complete in the form of charts, graphs, and the like, be sure to take the extra step to *interpret* the results. This will require previewing the results with different people knowledgeable about the organization and its people to pull out more contextual understanding. For example, there may be a specific reason why staff from one department feel strongly about a particular issue, maybe as a result of a recent project that went off the rails. Put on your detective hat and dig for clues when results don't quite add up or appear inconclusive.

Share responsibly. In some cases, it may be appropriate and useful to simply share the survey results with all staff once they're ready. But tread carefully here. There may be hidden triggers in the results that will serve to inflame strong feelings or cause shame or embarrassment among those that feel responsible for contributing to negative conditions. In such cases, it may be useful to check in or collaborate with knowledgeable colleagues to craft a delivery of results that will set a positive tone for what's to come. The objective is not to sugarcoat, but to strike a balance between an accurate representation of the present state and an avoidance of rubbing salt in longstanding wounds.

Stay Mindful of Your Mindset

While you and others conduct these discovery activities, they will likely inspire many ideas about how the challenges you uncover should be addressed. Be mindful of how people's natural tendency to immediately jump into solutioning mode when confronted with problems can derail the effort. Remembering the Beginner's Mindset from earlier in this book, try to suspend the urge to solve problems based on your own knowledge and experience, at least for now.

Some things to keep in mind:

Be open-minded. Don't assume you know that the first solution that pops into your head is the right one. You're here to learn. Bring an attitude of open curiosity. The time for co-designing solutions with those who will benefit from them most comes later.

Drop the jargon. Use of IT jargon during discussions and within project-related communication can make people feel disoriented and even unqualified to provide thoughts on enterprise technology. Instead, use the language most familiar to the interviewee. It may involve some prep work, but also try to incorporate their familiar terminology, such as terms relating to their department's business processes and tools, into the discussion.

Don't stick to the script. The interview guide should be just that – a guide! It does not need to be followed verbatim. Let the conversation flow naturally rather than reading from the script and go where there is interest and useful insights. Always probe further where you have a sense there is something more to be uncovered.

Listen actively. This may seem obvious, but actively listen. Pay attention to tone and body language. Ask follow-up questions to get down to the real meaning or embrace an awkward silence! It can encourage someone to finish their thought or reflect further on what was just said. If you are just waiting to ask the next question, people will sense that and shut down.

We can look to psychologists for tips on how to ask questions to get the best responses. And no, it doesn't have to be "How does that make you feel?"

Avoid "yes/no" answers. "Do you frequently use System A?" could get a yes or no answer, so reframe as a question designed for discussion, such as "Describe your experience of using System A." This will maximize insights. Ask for real-world examples or step-by-step walkthroughs, because people usually provide more detail and nuance in response to this type of question.

Don't lead the witness. "What don't you like about System A?" assumes they don't like it. "Tell me about your experience using System A" is open-ended *and* doesn't assign a sentiment. Also, avoid mentioning potential solutions. Maybe you think a specific application could solve your company's file management problems, but instead ask, "How could we improve file management?" It's important not to hinder thinking at this point because you're still gathering information.

As you wrap up the interview or focus group, leave time for any blue-sky ideas or anything else people want to share. If you can spark excitement about the prospect of improving your organization's digital workspace, the people you interview may be the people who will ultimately champion the resulting change effort.

Dream big. At the end of the session, ask what an ideal future state would look like. Even if their wish list seems impossible, write it down. Narrowing down ideas comes later; now is the time for brainstorming and thinking big. There are no wrong answers.

Share what to expect. Share immediate next steps and longer-term goals. You don't want interviewees to feel this was a dead-end exercise. You're building a coalition of digital transformation allies, one interview at a time, and you want their interest and support at every step along the way. Now is the time to start building trust and mutual understanding.

Actually follow up, and share findings. You'll continue to want their input, so be sure to circle back at an appropriate point in time to share and validate what you learned and talk about what you plan to do next.

Qualitative versus Quantitative Research and Analysis

The act of discovery is heavily reliant on what are traditionally referred to as qualitative research methods. The term *qualitative research* refers to a type of research designed to collect a subject's experience, perceptions, and behaviors through open-ended questions. This is in contrast to *quantitative research*, which is focused on collecting numerical data, usually through a structured instrument such as a survey that provides a limited choice of answers, often using a multiple-choice question format. While both methods can be used for your discovery and analysis, you'll find that qualitative research has much more to offer in terms of gaining a more nuanced understanding of staff challenges and unmet needs. Ideally, you will use quantitative research approaches sparingly, to get a general reading on trends, feelings, and behaviors, and then use qualitative research to delve deeper.

Surveys can be designed to gather both quantitative and qualitative data but their utility for collecting qualitative data is generally limited. For instance, you could have a survey question like the following:

How much time do you spend each day looking for the information you need to perform your work?

   a. Less than 30 minutes
   b. Between 30 minutes and 1 hour
   c. More than 1 hour

Or an open-ended question like this:

Briefly explain the challenges you encounter when looking for data or information you need to perform your work

In the first question, results can be neatly charted on a graph and will provide one view into the problem at hand but with no actionable details. The second question will hopefully produce details on the particular aspects of what people are struggling with and will therefore be more actionable than the first. Taken together, they will provide a rich, multidimensional view of the current reality.

But this is still not the whole picture. If you were to pose the second question during a live interview or focus group, you could probe more deeply to get the story behind what people are saying. People tend to provide very concise and somewhat surface-level responses to write-in questions in a survey, hence its limitation as a qualitative data collection method. Bottom line: human-to-human interaction is always best for collecting qualitative data, but surveys can be a quick method for taking the pulse of large swaths of the organization when time is tight or reaching people across the organization "face to face" will be challenging.

As I alluded to earlier, analysis of qualitative data is a relatively straightforward. In fact, many survey tools do this work for you, producing word clouds and even AI-generated summaries of write-in questions. But even here, there is one additional step: interpretation. Data interpretation is the act of looking at an analysis of the data and then making sense of it based on an understanding of the people and the underlying conditions that may have influenced their answers. This is where things get interesting, and where a little additional effort on your part will go a long way.

An effective method for qualitative data interpretation is to gather knowledgeable people together to review and discuss the research results, both qualitative and quantitative. During this exercise, the goal is to extract deeper meaning from the results analysis, and ultimately to tell a story about what the results mean and how they should be used. Once you've gathered these insights and discussion points, you're ready to present the results alongside the thinking that they generated. This will prevent people snoozing through your presentation and may even lead to the occasional aha moment or juicy discussion between those who disagree or have additional insights to offer.

Remember: first analyze, then interpret. For qualitative data, we're all somewhat familiar with the pretty charts and graphs and are relatively easy to produce. But what does analysis look like for qualitative data?

When it comes to analyzing qualitative data, there's no getting around the fact that it requires a deeper level of effort. While word clouds are fun to look at, they're not going to cut it for a serious review of information that could lead to major changes and investments. The next section provides a step-wise process you can use to move efficiently through the mountains of data you'll be collecting through focus groups and interviews, as well as those open-ended survey questions.

To Record or Not to Record

It is very common for qualitative researchers to record their interviews to facilitate notetaking and provide an artifact that can be referred back to if questions arise around a particular statement or detail shared. It is also an incredibly useful device where the one conducting the interview or focus group is working alone. As anyone who has tried knows, conducting a meaningful discussion while probing for details and nuances *and* taking detailed notes is about as easy as juggling eight balls at once.

So while there are many good reasons to record your interviews, I would urge you to stop and think about what, if any, negative repercussions there might be. For example, employees expressing their strong negative feelings about particular aspects of the organization's IT landscape or the people responsible for it may feel particularly vulnerable or uncomfortable about sharing their honest feelings if the session is being recorded. Even with the assurance that "this will not be shared," you may still encounter some hesitation. As with all things, use your best judgment and do what's necessary. It may be appropriate to record some sessions and not others. When you ask people's consent to record at the beginning of the session (and you must *always* get explicit consent), stay alert for people's discomfort. If it feels like it's going to create more distance and you can get away with notetaking, you might want to skip the recording for that particular session. Or if you can, have a notetaker on hand while you conduct every session so the option of not recording is always a comfortable option.

Getting Ready for Discovery Data Collection

Staying organized throughout the discovery process is critical. And as it always goes with staying organized, it's how you start that's key. You'll want to maintain a consistent process for notetaking, as well as for how you record, code, and analyze your findings. This will make analysis much less time-consuming when it comes time to make sense out of everything you have collected.

Before you begin gathering people's views, set up your data collections and analysis instruments. First, where will you record your interview notes? It doesn't really matter what you use, whether it's an electronic notepad, document, or something else, but it's important to use the same method throughout the process. Then make sure to save these notes in an organized fashion. At a minimum, title the notes for each session with the date it was conducted and a recognizable name for the event that you will also record in your discovery tracker.

The discovery tracker will be the electronic brain of your discovery work. It should include all key information related to your discovery so you can quickly reference it at any stage before, during, or after the project. The tracker can take a variety of forms, although I strongly suggest a spreadsheet or simple database. Ideally the format you choose will support cross-referencing of cell entries or values. (This will make more sense later, so don't worry if this sounds confusing!)

Additionally, I highly recommend including the IT systems inventory you collected in a previous exercise, as a separate tab or column in the tracker you'll use for collecting and analyzing the qualitative results. This will allow you to cross reference or link IT systems to the challenges or statements that are generated during your interviews and focus groups, and then tally the number of challenges, etc. belonging to each IT system.

Creating the Discovery Tracker

The discovery tracker is the main tool for collecting and analyzing the data you collect during the discovery process. Make sure to save it in a secure location where all of your key collaborators can access and add to it as needed. Since it contains potentially sensitive information, such as tracing viewpoints back to specific groups or individuals, be sure to limit access to only those who are directly involved in the discovery effort.

Suggested types of information to be housed in the discovery tracker are listed below. If using a spreadsheet or similar format, consider organizing and grouping the fields or columns across multiple tabs or tables to keep everything neat and manageable. If using an application where field types can be predefined, I've suggested field types for each in parentheses.

Suggested Information Categories and Fields

Tab/Table 1: IT systems inventory

Paste the IT systems inventory here so it can be cross-referenced in other sections as needed.

Tab/Table 2: Challenges

List unique challenges mentioned during discovery research. Suggested columns include:

- **Challenge (long text):** Provide a brief description of the challenge.
- **Type (single choice select):** Category field describing the general nature of the challenge. I generally use the following categories: people/culture, process, technology. Using a small number of categories will produce a nice graphic (e.g. pie chart or similar) showing the proportion of challenges that fall into each of these buckets.
- **Interviews (multi-select or text):** The actual interview(s) or focus group(s) where this challenge was mentioned. If you have the ability, generate a picklist from the list of interviews. Otherwise, simply type the name of the interview into a text field.
- **IT systems (multi-select or text):** IT systems that are related to this challenge. If you have the ability, generate a multi-picklist from the IT systems inventory in Table 1. Otherwise, simply type the name of the IT system(s) into a text field.
- **Quotes (long text):** Quotes (unattributed, of course!) can be a very powerful summation of people's feelings

(Continued)

(Continued)

and perceptions and make for good presentation content. Be sure to grab the good ones and list them here next to the challenge(s) they relate to.

Tab/Table 3: Opportunities

This is where you will record everything that might present an opportunity for your planned initiative. It could be an adjacent or complementary project, such as the replacement of an aging business system, or a new organizational strategy. If it potentially represents an opportunity to propel digital transformation in some way, note it down. It might be an important factor contributing to the effort's success.

- **Opportunity (text):** Present a brief description of the opportunity.
- **Interviews (multi-select or text):** The actual interview(s) or focus group(s) where this challenge was mentioned. If you have the ability, this is where linking to your list of interviews in Tab/Table 4 (see below) will be helpful to generate a picklist. Otherwise, simply type the name of the interview into a text field.
- **IT systems (multi-select or text):** Any IT systems that are related to this challenge. If you have the ability, this is where linking to your IT systems inventory in Table 1 will be helpful to generate a picklist. Otherwise, simply type the name of the interview into a text field.
- **Quotes (long text):** Quotes (unattributed, of course!) can be a very powerful summation of people's feelings and perceptions and make for good presentation content. Be sure to grab the good ones and list them here next to the challenge(s) they relate to.

Tab/Table 4: Interviews

This is where you list all the interviews that were conducted. It will be important to keep track of when these were held and who took part. You can then use this information to populate the "Interviews" field within the "Challenges" and "Opportunities" tabs or tables.

◆ **Interview or focus group name (text):** Provide simple descriptive title of the session, such as "Interview with Latisha Warner."

◆ **Date (date):** Indicate the date the session took place.

◆ **[Optional] Facilitator(s) (text or multi-select):** If it's important to track who conducted the session; note it here.

◆ **Participants (text or multi-select):** List all the people who took part in the session. If possible, pull in these names from the list of participants in Tab/Table 5 (see below).

◆ **Meeting notes (hyperlink):** Link to the meeting notes document and/or recording or transcripts so that you can easily refer when needed.

Tab/Table 5: Interviewees

This is where you will keep the master list of all the people you spoke with. This information is important so that you can maintain a record of everyone who participated, check that you've gotten the desired levels of representation from different staff categories, and to communicate to stakeholders about where the information being used to drive the initiative came from. In this way, you can demonstrate the validity of the findings, especially if there is disagreement about their substance.

◆ **Full Name (text):** Full name of each participant
◆ **Title (text):** Their job title
◆ **Department (text):** Their department
◆ **Seniority (text or single-select):** The level of their role within the organization, typically includes things like C-suite, VP, department lead, mid-level, junior, or other designations that make sense for your organization.

(Continued)

(Continued)

♦ **Office or location (text or single-select):** Office or geographic location in which they're based

Other potentially useful information, based on the criteria used to select participants and/or the ways in which your organization ensured participation of diverse voices and perspectives, could include the following:

♦ Race/ethnicity
♦ Gender
♦ Primary language
♦ Age group

Prepare the Discussion Guide

As mentioned earlier, the discussion guide is just that – a guide – so don't get caught up in writing 30 questions that you will have to blaze through in a 60-minute focus group. Instead, focus on the general topics that matter most and provide the interviewer with reminders and prompts on where and when to go deeper. Ideally the interviewer will be experienced or knowledgeable enough to know when there is more information below the surface to be gathered, and when to move on to the next question. The following is a sample guide format that I've used successfully with many clients. You know your organization best, as well as the particular realities you're trying to uncover, so take the time to create a set of well-considered questions that will produce the most valuable information.

SAMPLE INTERVIEW OR FOCUS GROUP DISCUSSION GUIDE

Session Introduction
Talking points that introduce the purpose of the discussion, the people leading the initiative, how this information will be used and shared, and any other pertinent information

Focus Group Ground Rules Some general rules for how to engage in the session – only necessary when more than two to three people are

participating in the session. Modify the following generic rules to suit your culture and audience.

To help ensure that everyone actively takes part in today's conversation and to keep us on track, here are a few suggested ground rules or agreements. What do you all think?

- There are no right or wrong answers, only differing points of view.
- One person speaks at a time.
- You don't need to agree with others, but please listen respectfully as others share their views.
- Turn off your cellphones or turn your cellphone on to vibrate; close other devices or windows.
- If virtual, we encourage you to keep your camera on to fully engage in the conversation; however, if you need to turn your camera off at any point, this is okay.
- If you must respond to a call, please do so as quietly as possible and rejoin us as quickly as you can.
- My role as moderator will be to guide the discussion and ensure we hear from all participants.
- We will be recording this focus group conversation for note-taking purposes; the recording will not be shared. Do I have your consent to record?

Discussion Questions

The following question formats are for example only; please take time to think about what will yield the right level and type of information to drive your efforts.

1. Please briefly introduce yourself and explain your role, including your title and department.
2. A goal of this project is to make it easier for staff to [explain one or more anticipated outcomes of the digital transformation work]:
   a. Which IT systems do you primarily use for these activities?
   b. What challenges are you currently experiencing related to these activities?
   c. Where do you turn when you have difficulty?
   d. What specific improvements (technology or process) would you like to see in this area?

3. What is the one thing you want to see change and/or improve from this effort?

4. What is your biggest concern, or what do you see as the biggest risk, in relation to this effort?

5. What else would you like to mention that we haven't touched on?

Closing Talking Points

Thank you again for your time today.

You will receive updates as this work progresses with additional opportunities to share your perspective. If you have additional questions or suggestions at any time, you can send them to [project point of contact].

Your Assignment

♦ It's time to start listening! First, think about the people you will want to include in one or more discovery activities. This doesn't have to be an exhaustive list. As you speak with people, they will likely suggest others who should be included in the process, but try to generate an initial list that covers the diversity or staff roles and perspectives most important to the work areas you will be investigating. Use a spreadsheet for this purpose, with columns devoted to the selection criteria you deem most important. (You can transfer this information into the discovery tracker once you've made your final participant selections.) Suggested columns include:

- Name
- Department
- Job function (operations, work area, etc.)
- Seniority (junior, middle management, executive, etc.)
- Years at organization (less than 1, 1–5, more than 5)
- Office and/or geographic location
- Worker type (in-office, hybrid, fully remote, field-based, etc.)

It might be useful to select participants in collaboration with key project stakeholders, and perhaps others who have a deep understanding of your organization's people and dynamics. It's easy to get stuck in groupthink here, so don't leave out valuable perspectives from outside the immediate project team.

◆ Once you've identified people to take part in your research, develop the discussion guide. If you're conducting both one-on-one interviews and focus groups, you may find that the questions can be quite similar or the same for both. In some cases, it may make sense to reserve one-on-one interviews for people with particularly strong points of view, key roles in the process(es) under review, or leaders or others who will feel more comfortable expressing their views in private.

For focus groups, it may make sense to group people together who share similar roles or who play complementary roles in a particular business process being examined. In some cases, you may want to group people together based on their level of comfort expressing their perspectives – such as recent new hires who may find it easier to share their thoughts among other new hires versus more tenured staff in their department, including those they report to.

As you develop your interview guide, keep in mind that this is a guide and not a script. You will want it to cover the topics and areas of exploration, as well as important prompts for diving deeper into the underlying thoughts and feelings of those being interviewed. But it will also be important to remain somewhat flexible during these sessions so that there is space to explore on-the-spot discoveries or delve deeper into issues you may not have anticipated. After all, that is what true listening is all about!

(Continued)

(Continued)

- Last but not least, it's time to gather what you heard and analyze it using the discovery tracker. You may find it easiest to "code as you go" – in other words, enter the data that you need to collect after you or others conduct each interview or focus group and while the discussions are fresh in the minds of those who led them.

CHAPTER 7

Envisioning

Transformation requires a clear vision in addition to planning and strategy. It will be important to rally the organization around a shared vision for the future that authentically represents what people want and need while remaining realistic in terms of what the organization can practically achieve. Of course, to make the case for digital transformation to your organization, you'll also need a clear, high-level vision and a set of objectives that can inspire and mobilize others. Armed with these items, together with the information you generated during the discovery phase, you'll have everything you could possibly need to move forward.

Envisioning what will be possible once your digital transformation effort has achieved its objectives is by far the most powerful and important stage of the digital transformation journey. Just like Loyce and I discovered in Kenya, dreaming and intention-setting comes first. Once the vision is clear, getting from here to there is just a matter of figuring out the steps (and time, money, and energy) required.

When it comes to organizational change, dreams about the future cannot be developed in a vacuum. It takes a village to crystallize a vision for the future that people can buy into and get excited about. And then there are the considerations around the realities of time, money, and organizational priorities. The trick is to create a shared vision both collaboratively and rapidly so as not to lose project momentum. The last thing you want is for the idea of co-creating a shared vision to be confused with reaching consensus. The latter will happen when it needs to but could end up stalling the project indefinitely if attempted too soon.

The Future-State Workshop

In this chapter we'll discuss how to create a shared vision of the future using what I call the Future-State Vision Workshop format. These workshops are an opportunity to bring people together from across the organization to develop a digital transformation vision and clear sense of desired outcomes. Once this step is complete, you will be fully on the path to manifesting the ideal digital workplace.

This exercise is a chance to step beyond the current-state challenges and technological realities you uncovered previously and jump into the realm of the possible. Through this, you will discover people's ideas and aspirations for what role technology could and should play in supporting their work.

The Future-State Vision Workshop is also an opportunity to identify which dreams are realistic, and which are just, well, only dreams. One of the downsides of the never-ending tech hype cycle is that tech companies are often promising far more than they can deliver. The less experienced or knowledgeable tech consumer can easily fall into the trap of believing the hype and then blaming those responsible for implementing new technology for falling short of their unrealistic expectations. This is particularly challenging when organizational leaders are among those who have drunk the proverbial tech-hype Kool Aid.

Keep these potential pitfalls in mind as you enter into conversations about the future, especially among those who control budgets and decisions affecting these efforts. Expectation setting at this stage is critical – among key stakeholders as well as among project team members – and the savvy planner will always aim to keep expectations low and then exceed them. I have seen many a digital transformation leader fall victim to their own wide-eyed enthusiasm, only to have it turned against them once the project's promises didn't live up to reality.

Building a Big Tent

Use this time as an opportunity to identify champions who can serve as partners and advocates throughout the remainder of the journey. And don't limit your selection to those who seem to be exactly on the same page as you. For instance, the naysayers with strong opinions can sometimes be converted into powerful allies, particularly when you are able to address their chief concerns and even adjust course to align more closely with their needs and concerns.

The thing about naysayers that people tend to overlook is that they actually care a lot about the outcomes, just not necessarily in the same way that you or your collaborators do. Look a little deeper to see if there's an opening to make a connection using your now well-oiled empathy skills. Naturally, some people take joy in being an opposing force for no matter what the situation. These are the people you need to look out for because they will continue to shift the goal post of their dissatisfaction no matter how far backwards you bend. Trying to please or appease these folks will get you nowhere and leave you exhausted and dismayed. On the other hand, some may be skeptical for good reason, whether based on previous bad experiences with tech, a general distrust of "this type of thing," or more specific opposition to the focus or aims of the digital transformation effort. For these people, you may find that once you acknowledge and capably address their concerns, a loyal ally will emerge.

Now is also the time to set a tone for what's to come. Transparency and a spirit of open collaboration is key. With organizational initiatives as significant as the one you're leading, it's tempting to wield your power in forceful or dismissive ways. This could take the form of ignoring people who raise objections or of restricting access to information to those who don't "play ball." If you feel tensions starting to rise within or outside your circle of collaborators, it may be time to conduct a health check. Is there some control that you could loosen

(Continued)

(Continued)

to help people on the fringes feel more included or heard? Is there information you could share with the organization more broadly, even if ideas aren't fully baked or plans laid in stone? While it might seem counterintuitive, revealing the fluid, fluctuating nature of the discovery and planning process can comfort those who tend to fear deterministic, top-down decisions that hit them unawares.

Selecting Workshop Participants

Just like you did during the "Listening" step, choose a diverse range of participants from different roles and experience levels. But unlike listening, when it is sometimes preferable to hear from groups of people that share something in common, here it is generally best to encourage cross-pollination of differing ideas and perspectives.

Each workshop, whether virtual or in-person, should have no more than 15–20 participants. If you are at a larger organization, you may choose to host several workshops over a short time frame so that an adequate cross-section of people can take part.

You will also want to recruit one or two colleagues to help co-facilitate the workshop. Ideas will be coming in fast, so you'll want to stay on top of what's being shared while keeping the conversation moving.

Invites should be sent at least two weeks in advance and should include some questions that people can think about ahead of time. Here's a sample invitation message:

Join us on [DATE] for a **Future-State Vision Workshop** to generate ideas about how we can transform the state of our technology to be happier and more productive at work.

During this 90-minute interactive session, we will generate answers to the question "What would working here be like if our technology was [better aligned with/better able to support] key business goals and processes?"

In preparation, please reflect on the following two questions:

1. How could or should the nature of our work improve with the help of technology?
2. What types of [business, employee experience, other] specific outcomes would be achieved if we successfully advance the state of our technology?

Planning the Workshop

When developing your workshop agenda, create space for the free flow of ideas and interaction of participants. This workshop should not feel overly structured or restrictive.

Since this is the beginning of a conversation around the potential focus and benefits of digital transformation, set a tone of "anything goes" so people feel safe to be bold and imaginative. You never know what kind of unexpected ideas might turn up.

Try to avoid getting too "in the weeds" on specific system features or functionality. If these come up, put them in the parking lot and pull back to the bigger picture discussion. It's not yet time for "solutioning."

A sample 90-minute agenda is presented below.

Sample Future-State Vision Workshop

Time (minutes)	Workshop Activity
10	**Welcome to Our Future–State Vision Workshop** Recap the objectives and current status of the digital transformation effort and the purpose of the workshop.
20	**Part 1: Art of the Possible** Share examples of ways that your organization or others have transformed their work with the help of technology. Then discuss some of the real-world capabilities of technology that you have or are thinking of acquiring, but is not yet available to the organization or being used effectively. This will help educate participants about what's possible, while grounding their vision within the frame of realistic expectations

(Continued)

(Continued)

Time (minutes)	Workshop Activity
20	**Part 2: Craft "How Might We" Questions** Now it's time to transform these possibilities into actionable statements. Have participants phrase a series of questions that begin with the phrase "How might we . . ." For example, "How might we reduce our turnaround times on new contract approvals?"
20	**Part 3: Imagine the Future** Now fast-forward to the post-digital transformation future where these capabilities are now in place (for now, skip over how to get there). Brainstorm what benefits staff members, teams, partners, and the organization as a whole will experience. Prompt people to think about business benefits but also happiness-at-work benefits, such as more positive staff interactions or lower rates of burnout. Color coding may be useful here as well to categorize similar or related outcomes into "buckets."
15	**Part 4: Identify Considerations and Next Steps** Ask the group about any anticipated risks or barriers they think stand in the way of moving forward with achieving the envisioned future state. Keep it high level; you'll have chances to delve deeper as the project continues. Ask about any further conversations or participants that people feel will contribute to the discussion.
5	**Wrap-Up and Thank You** Thank participants for being part of the workshop. Share what's next for the project and how they will be kept involved and informed moving forward.

Following the workshop, use a new section of the Discovery Tracker you created during the previous chapter to gather and analyze what you heard. Suggested columns or fields for this new "Future Vision" tab are as follows:

- **Design question:** List all of the "how might we" questions generated during the workshop.
- **Category:** Create meaningful categories based on the natural groupings the questions fall into. These could include things like business process, system enhancement, system change, culture, and so on.
- **Expected benefits:** Add the expected benefits mentioned by participants that relate to each design question. It is likely

that these will be repeated across multiple questions; that's okay. You may want to further divide these into an individual/ employee benefits category and an organizational benefits category.

♦ **Risks/barriers:** Add potential risks or barriers mentioned by participants that related to each design question. You may want to further divide these into categories based on type. Again, it is expected that these will repeat across different questions.

Presenting the Vision

As you prepare your presentation on the future-state vision, consider who you are presenting to. Tailor your message and language to the individuals in the room to proactively address their concerns while highlighting their areas of interest. The goal is to convince them that the digital transformation project is a necessary investment so you can ask for what you need to embark on the next step of the digital transformation journey. If there is already agreement on the overarching goals of the project, now is an opportunity to begin building buy-in for the specific types of change that will be needed.

You will want to synthesize all that you have learned and developed over the course of the previous activities using the following Future-State Vision Presentation Outline provided as a guide. The outline includes standard background information on digital transformation (definition, organizational value) as well as prompts for organization-specific information about your current state of technology, discovery analysis, objectives and strategic alignment, future-state vision, and high-level budget. Spend sufficient time on this presentation to ensure it is clear, comprehensive, and persuasive.

One of the key components of the Future-State Vision Presentation that you will have a chance to create at this stage is the future-state technology map. It will be provisional at this stage but is an important tool for helping people picture what changes will be required to achieve the vision being set forth. To develop this map, I suggest you sit with members of the project team as well as other key advisors with a deep knowledge of the current tech stack. Together, walk through the synthesized discovery findings as well as the Future-State Vision Workshop outputs. Once everyone is fully read into what has been learned up to this moment, it's *finally* time to start solutioning. If you have consultants involved, this is a moment where they should be able to contribute a lot of value.

Begin by looking at the current-state tech map and inventory you prepared during Chapter 5. If meeting in person, I suggest projecting the map on a wall so it really comes to life. If virtual, this can be done via screen share. Marshalling the collective experience and wisdom in the real or virtual "room," combined with a deep understanding and regard for what has been learned to date, start the process of determining what can be done to move the organization toward the desired future state. Think about the tech changes that will do one or more of the following to help you get started building the future-state map:

- ◆ Reduce duplication and overlap of features or functionality.
- ◆ Reduce system cost and/or complexity.
- ◆ Introduce meaningful connections (i.e. integrations or automations) to address business process inefficiencies.
- ◆ Eliminate unofficial or "shadow" systems.

Once you have done a first pass at the map, keep iterating based on what "makes sense" to the group. Remember that this is a *provisional* map so there is no need to get it perfect just yet. The goal is to introduce meaningful changes that the team believes will address many priority needs while helping achieve some of the overarching digital transformation objectives. You can use this version of the map as a visual prototype of sorts, using it to gather feedback and reactions from various stakeholders to gauge how well received, or not, certain proposed changes might be received in different parts of the organization.

When you begin developing the digital transformation roadmap in later chapters, you'll have plenty of opportunity to keep iterating on this map and begin defining the people and process-related changes that will be needed to support the outcomes that technology cannot support alone.

Creating the Future-State Vision Presentation

The Future-State Vision Presentation will be a critical tool for increasing understanding and buy-in for the changes that will lead to a healthier and more productive digital workplace. As with any presentation, you'll want to present the information clearly and concisely, tailored to your specific audience(s), and built on the assumption that not everyone who sees it will be intimately familiar with the overall digital transformation effort.

Here is a suggested presentation outline to get you started:

- ◆ Project background
  - Staff involved
  - Date started and objectives
  - Goals
  - Alignment with organizational strategies and values

- ◆ Current state of technology
  - Major pain points
  - Areas of opportunity
  - Current-state technology map

- ◆ Future-state technology vision
  - Summary of the Future-State Vision Workshop, including "how might we" design questions, expected benefits, and risks
  - Provisional future-state technology map showing a suggested technology approach to achieve the desired future state
  - Priority pain points to be addressed
  - Systems changed or eliminated and justifications
  - Systems added and justifications
  - Cost analysis, including breakdown of anticipated cost savings over time

(Continued)

(Continued)

◆ Steps to achieving the future-state vision
  ● Change management approach
  ● Leadership support
  ● Staff involvement
  ● Expected impact
  ● Proposed time frames
  ● Proposed budget

Finally, when it comes to making a good presentation, make sure to build in time for rich discussion. This is far more effective than breathlessly ending a rushed monologue with 30 seconds to spare. The presentation will likely provide a lot of new information for your audience to absorb, so give them the time and space to reflect and ask questions. You may even want to share the presentation with them a few days beforehand so they can come prepared.

Keep in mind that although this presentation is an important step in gaining support, it is not the last. Even if you leave without the pledge of support you were hoping for, don't get discouraged. In some cases, building up support will require multiple conversations, especially when the project is somewhat new or not widely understood. Better to let ideas settle in gradually than bombard people with too many details that they are not ready for.

Once you receive initial buy-in on moving ahead, we recommend sharing the presentation as broadly as possible (perhaps minus the financial slides; you know your organizational culture best). This is a foundational document that can be used to build a shared understanding of digital transformation and what it means for your organization. You can also simplify the presentation or share excerpts in an all-staff meeting or communication, possibly followed by a Q&A. The importance of keeping all employees plugged in and engaged as the effort rolls ahead cannot be overstated.

Your Assignment

♦ Host one or more future-state workshops using the approach outlined with select staff to begin building a shared vision of the future. Try to conduct these workshops within the shortest time frame possible to avoid losing project momentum.

♦ Create and use the new section of the discovery tracker to record your findings. As in previous synthesis, make sure to link participant contributions to specific IT systems, challenges, and opportunities from existing sections of the discovery tracker. Consider adding another category, "business processes," to the discovery tracker to help you zero in on which business processes stand to benefit most from the envisioned changes, while taking note of business processes that were either intentionally omitted or overlooked.

♦ If desired, present your findings in summary form to those who participated in the discovery research and future-state workshop to validate and collect feedback on the findings.

♦ Prepare and present the Future-State Vision Presentation. Present it first to key stakeholders, including key decision-makers. Based on the feedback you receive, and with the blessing of those involved, you may want to present an abbreviated version to a wider group of stakeholders or the organization at large. Remember that transparency at this stage, and throughout this process, is critical. By sharing the thoughts, assumptions, and ideas that are feeding into the final plan, you are justifying the need for this effort while building support for what's to come.

PART III

Achieving the Ideal
Digital Workplace

"Simple can be harder than complex: You have to work hard to get your thinking clean to make it simple. But it's worth it in the end because once you get there, you can move mountains."
— Steve Jobs

At this stage you've gathered a wide variety of employee perspectives regarding their needs and wants and established a preliminary shared vision for the future state of the digital enterprise. Along the way, you and your collaborators have hopefully made some discoveries about how the mix and configuration of your digital tools can be redesigned in ways that will support better ways of working and connecting across the organization. Nicely done! Everything you've achieved up to this point will put you on a path to building a truly human-centered digital workplace.

Now comes the fun part of designing the digital transformation approach in detail. Here I'd like to introduce another Zen-inspired concept: simplicity. As we've all discovered over the course of the digital revolution over the last half century, achieving simplicity of our digital environment takes effort. In other words, if we stand by passively and let the technology (and those who sell it) dictate how we select and work with it, we will soon be surrounded by a chaotic and cluttered mess of tools that feels anything but simple.

Most of us, like Steve Jobs, understand that achieving simplicity is difficult. Anyone who has tried to edit a 10-page document down to 1 page knows this. And I'd be willing to wager that most of us prefer the simple over the complex. This was likely a common refrain among those you interviewed about their digital tools. But we are products of a consumer-driven society who habitually acquire shiny new things with the hope that the things themselves will solve our problems. Deep down we know this is wrong thinking. But to approach it in another way would take more time and humility than most of us have to spare. This is particularly acute in the workplace, because there is often a blurred line of accountability when it comes to technology decision-making. If the technology inevitably fails to solve the underlying problem, it's seen as the fault of the technology, not a lack of intentionality around how the digital workplace was designed.

The systems mapping exercise you completed earlier likely highlighted the degree to which your digital workplace has grown alarmingly complex. Common challenges you might have observed include the presence of several tools that perform the same thing in slightly different ways, systems that don't "talk" to each other despite supporting the same or closely related business processes, and the presence of outdated legacy systems that have yet to be decommissioned because they house valuable data that hasn't yet been given a new home. By embarking on a journey to mindfully redesign the digital enterprise, just as this book's title suggests, you will be able to reduce and refine the digital environment into its simplest and, dare I say, most beautiful form for the benefit of all who interact with it.

CHAPTER 8

The Art of Digital Decluttering

Back to Marie Kondo and the concept of tidying. I call this chapter "The Art of Digital Decluttering" because, like anything that is meant to "spark joy" as Marie Kondo puts it, the design of the digital workplace must be an intentional, creative act. It seems obvious when you think about it, yet I have rarely seen a digital workplace that I would characterize as being intentionally designed, or creative. Much like the homes Marie Kondo visits, they are simply an accumulation of what could be called digital clutter. Applications purchased, half configured, and abandoned like the trousers you wore only once and never took off the hanger again. Powerful new systems where only 10% of the available functionality has been deployed, much like unworn shoes still in the box. And old decrepit systems that have been customized to the hilt and repaired so many times that the people who originally developed them are well into retirement, much like ill-fitting hand-me-downs that we hesitate to throw or give away.

And that's not even getting into the content stored in these systems. (We could dedicate an entire book to that!) But suffice it to say, an overstuffed closet would be an analogy too kind for the type of clutter that exists in most electronic databases and file repositories. Just like Kondo's clients, the owners or inheritors of these systems are filled with anxiety and embarrassment about the state of things, yet feel incapable of doing anything about it.

Where to begin? Just like Marie Kondo, we need some rules that will guide us on our decluttering mission. Having a systematic approach will reduce the level of anxiety and overwhelm that we feel, especially at the beginning of the process. Once we're confidently moving forward, momentum will take care of the rest!

The Basic Rules of (Digital) Tidying

Marie Kondo's method employs what she refers to as the "6 Basic Rules of Tidying." They are: commit yourself to tidying up; imagine your ideal lifestyle; finish discarding first; tidy by category, not location; follow the right order; and ask yourself if it sparks joy.

SARA'S RULES FOR DIGITAL TIDYING

While Kondo's rules are great when applied to messy households, they aren't exactly right for the digital enterprise (sorry, Marie!). So I've taken her rules and put an alternative spin on these very important concepts so that you can easily use them to declutter your organization's digital landscape.

- ◆ Rule #1 Be clear and unified on the end goal.
- ◆ Rule #2 Imagine the ideal digital employee experience.
- ◆ Rule #3 Subtract before adding.
- ◆ Rule #4 Streamline systems by business process, not system type.
- ◆ Rule #5 Start downstream and work your way up.
- ◆ Rule #6 Aim for employee happiness.

Rule #1: Be Clear and Unified on the End Goal

Many goals may be fueling your organization's digital transformation journey: greater efficiency, employee retention, IT restructuring, cost savings, process improvement, and more. To ensure the effort stays focused and can be deemed a success, there should be consensus on the specific outcomes that will make it all worthwhile. This will also avoid misunderstandings or dashed expectations. For example, achieving greater efficiency through improved technology and lowering IT costs may or may not be correlated, depending on the approach taken. If there is agreement that cost savings trumps greater efficiency, then there won't be disappointment when efficiency flatlines or even dips because of these changes. Make sure the goalposts are clear and agreed upon by all who will evaluate the effort's ultimate success.

Rule #2: Imagine the Ideal Digital Employee Experience

Without getting too bogged down in the current state of your digital tools, what would the ideal digital employee experience look like for your organization? Which business processes would be easier? Where would efficiency gains free up staff to engage in other, higher-value activities? Would people be enjoying their work life more, and would workplace stress decrease? How about reducing friction between departments that share different phases of a linked process? Continue to build a clear vision of the future with your project collaborators and other stakeholders, just like you started to do during the Future-State Vision Workshop discussed in Chapter 7. This vision, coupled with the clear end goals established under Rule #1, will keep the effort headed in the right direction while decreasing the risk that technology will overshadow the real human experiences it is meant to support and enhance.

Rule #3: Subtract Before Adding

Digital transformation efforts often focus on adding technology or technology-driven capabilities, whether through acquiring an entirely new system or enhancing an existing one. These days, due to the proliferation of enterprise tools, most organizations would benefit from a technology "haircut" involving the removal of superfluous or redundant technology, as well as unofficial or shadow IT applications. Making these reductions first, before any new technology is introduced, will not only create space for new systems but can help drive decisions around what capabilities and tools are truly needed.

When abiding by this rule, it's important to acknowledge that this approach will require patience, often beyond what the average digital transformation leader can or will exercise. But sometimes, as I'm known to say, we need to slow down to speed up. As the streamlined digital workplace begins to take shape in the absence of outdated and overlapping tech, the value of being able to see and think clearly should be apparent.

Rule #4: Streamline Systems by Business Process, Not System Type

It might be tempting to try to reduce the number of systems occupying each category within your IT systems inventory. While it may seem problematic to have, say, two CRMs or three instant messaging platforms, there may be entirely good reasons for this duplication. To avoid reducing your tech footprint in ways that disrupt more than enhance, pay careful attention to the key business processes you are intent on improving and look at the ways in which people supporting these processes interact with the various systems. If you take a critical piece of functionality away by removing one system, you'll have to replace it somehow (hence the importance of rule #3) and ideally streamline the process as a result. Bottom line, the puzzle may be more complex than you think. While simplicity is the goal, don't be oversimplistic in your tidying approach. Dig into the details of why and how people touch each system in the course of doing their work and then consider how to streamline and simplify without leaving people – and the business processes they support – hanging.

Rule #5: Start Downstream and Work Your Way Up

Think of the various information flows in your organization. Even when data appears to be "at rest," such as files residing in a cloud file server, it came from somewhere, and eventually it will go somewhere else. When thinking of where to start the decluttering process, starting downstream means starting where data enters into your digital environment and working your way upstream, eventually to the systems that produce outputs to be consumed – the end of the line, so to speak. This is not a hard and fast rule and there can be good reasons why cleanup in this order will not be feasible. In any case, thinking about your refreshed digital landscape from the bottom up can support more streamlined data flows across the organization.

Rule #6: Aim for Employee Happiness

With all the talk about efficiency and productivity when it comes to enterprise tech, it can be easy, especially for those most technologically inclined, to overlook the importance of employee well-being. Keep this outcome as the North Star of the digital transformation effort and it will be hard to fail. I am constantly surprised at the lengths people will go to get their work done in spite of the technology-related hurdles they encounter. These feats of heroism take their toll and eventually cause people to burn out. There are very real financial and social costs associated with employee burnout, which is reaching epidemic proportions just as the rate of change within the enterprise tech landscape goes exponential. I don't believe this is a coincidence. As humans, we struggle with unnecessary levels of complexity. We want to find the quickest and easiest route to achieve a given task; it's a key to our survival and it's probably baked into our DNA. To be forced to go about our work in ways that are counter to this instinct is to feel that we are failing. Let's build digital environments that create heroes, not martyrs.

■ ■ ■

With these rules in mind, you can now embark on the tidying process that will drive the planning around what tools wills be eliminated, kept but enhanced, or kept as they are. Once you have made some determinations of what changes will be most beneficial, especially to the digital employee experience overall, you are ready to begin planning the implementation of these changes.

CHAPTER 9

Selecting Timing and Tactics

"Right time, right place, right people equals success. Wrong time, wrong place, wrong people equals most of the real human history."

— Idries Shah

The success of any major project is largely dependent on two factors: timing and tactics. This is perhaps never truer than in the period leading up to the launch of your digital transformation implementation efforts. As you prepare to take your digital transformation project forward, reflect on the factors outside of your immediate sphere of activity that may help or hinder your efforts. Where is your organization in its budget cycle? Have strategic projects been defined for the coming year? Have improvements of certain components of your organization's tech stack already been designated as an organizational priority? These are some of the many factors to consider when it comes to determining the best timing.

While chances are you and your project collaborators are beginning to feel the urgency, don't rush into your project without first lining up the necessary internal support. Take the time to cultivate buy-in from leadership, ensure adequate bandwidth from key staff, and secure a budget. This process may take a while, but once these resources are secured, you'll be able to ramp up quickly.

If consensus is not yet reached among the organization's leaders that now is the time to move forward, you have some work left to do in this area. Certainly, the findings from your discovery work, together with a compelling future-state vision, can unlock a great deal of support. But there may be other current realities that can contribute to the sense of urgency. Perhaps the organization is being forced to upgrade an existing system or migrate to a new system from one that is being deprecated. The pressure of external competition may provide another source of motivation for investments in digital transformation. Do you need to catch up with industry leaders to remain relevant? Would better use of your digital tools give you a competitive advantage? These types of events can provide a perfect opportunity to combine forces and turn a mundane and even dreaded change into something truly transformational.

Choosing the right tactics is another key consideration. Consider what tactics will help you achieve the desired result before speeding ahead, consulting with those you trust to help you get it right. For example, a longer-term, phased approach to implementing changes may be preferable given budget constraints or change fatigue. In other cases, a more rapid, rip-the-Band-Aid approach will serve the organization better, given urgency and an anticipated high degree of employee cooperation. Whatever the case, the tactics you choose to implement the desired levels of change will be just as important as the changes themselves in achieving the project's intended results.

To help you anticipate the factors that will drive decisions around timing and tactics, I've provided the following Digital Transformation Readiness Assessment that you can use to uncover any obvious hurdles you'll need to clear before implementing planned changes. And yes, this should be done *before* you build out the Digital Transformation Roadmap that will contain the exact timing and tactics you will use. Thoughtfulness and proactive attention to detail will serve you well here.

The assessment questions are organized according to the following three "Bs":

Buy-in: Do you have the support of leadership? Although you'll need to assemble a cross-functional team of allies, executive sponsorship and engaged support are essential. Reach out to key leaders early to begin building your case, ideally timing any concrete requests prior to budget season.

Bandwidth: What other special projects or initiatives are in progress? Is there appetite and bandwidth for another? This is particularly important for smaller organizations if the same key stakeholders are tied up with other priorities. Moreover, what does your organization's workload look like throughout the year? Are there busier months (such as the fiscal year end, the holiday season, or the annual audit) that you should avoid for the kickoff of a cross-organizational initiative?

Budget: Is a budget already secured and is it realistic? Or will you have to go back for more once the work is under way? Perhaps there are savings that need to be spent by the end of the fiscal year, or maybe you need to get this project included in next year's budget. Consider your organization's budget cycle and be ready to plug in to that process early with realistic estimates to secure the dollars you need to get to the finish line.

Digital Transformation Readiness Assessment

Use this assessment to get an accurate read on how well equipped your organization is to take the next step on its digital transformation journey. You may find there are still areas that need attention before the next stage of work can begin.

Instructions: Rate each question in terms of how much you agree or disagree using the following options: strongly agree, agree, neither agree nor disagree, disagree, or strongly disagree.

Part 1: Buy-In

- There is a general consensus among leadership that technology improvements are needed.
- Enhanced technology has been identified as a strategic goal or priority, or one or more strategic goals or priorities will require enhanced technology.
- One or more members of the leadership team are likely sponsors or champions of the digital transformation effort.
- Our technology is felt by leadership to be negatively impacting our organization's performance and/or competitiveness.

Part 2: Bandwidth

- There are no other significant, company-wide initiatives under way or planned for the next year.
- We have staff members who have the needed knowledge and skills to lead and support all aspects of a digital transformation effort.
- Key staff needed to lead and support digital transformation will be able to dedicate adequate time to this effort.
- A cross-functional working group or committee focused on how our organization uses technology exists and can be enlisted to help guide this effort to completion.

Part 3: Budget

- We have budget set aside in the current or upcoming fiscal year to invest in digital transformation staff level-of-effort (LOE) and any related technology.
- Departments other than IT that have a stake in the digital transformation effort are willing and able to dedicate needed budget and/or staff time to ensure the project benefits from their active involvement and support.
- There is a mechanism in place to track and coordinate investments in the digital transformation effort across all organizational units that will contribute.
- We have a clear and compelling picture of the anticipated return on investment (ROI) that will be achieved through execution of the digital transformation project.

Once you have gathered your answers and collected answers from other key stakeholders if desired, review and notate what, if any actions are needed to address areas of outstanding need. Unless you've answered "agree" or "strongly agree" to the majority of these questions, there are still hurdles to be cleared before the implementation can or should begin.

Developing the Digital Transformation Roadmap

Once you have identified and begun to address any outstanding obstacles in your path, it's time to map out the next stage of the journey. As you do this, you'll want to focus on what you see as the best way forward. Some compromises will likely be required in terms of how far or fast you can run based on budgets and resource availability. For now, the focus is on building the most comprehensive and convincing picture of how needed changes will be implemented to alleviate the most pressing challenges that staff and the organization are facing.

The Digital Transformation Roadmap is a master plan for the changes that will be implemented over the coming months and years. While the roadmap can take numerous forms, from a Gantt-style project plan to a narrative document, the roadmap will serve several purposes. Perhaps most importantly, it will paint a clear picture of what digital transformation will look like at your organization. In doing this, it will help people better understand the practical implications of proposed changes and the specific challenges that the effort will address. It will also be a tool for communicating plans, at a high level, to decision-makers across the organization so that you can gather targeted feedback, guidance, and support. As the project progresses, plan to revisit the roadmap regularly to iterate on and adjust it based on changing priorities and needs. It is intended to be a "living" document that should always reflect the most accurate and up-to-date version of the digital transformation journey.

The roadmap content will reference much of the information gathered during the discovery (i.e. "Looking," "Listening," and "Envisioning") phases of the project. If you haven't already, you will want to take this opportunity to synthesize and distill this information, preferably together with collaborators and key stakeholders, before adding it to the roadmap. For example, think about the level of urgency around every challenge that emerged as a priority. Then weigh that against what you know about organizational priorities, the organization's tolerance for change, and what might be most likely to unearth previously hidden pockets of resistance.

A good roadmap serves multiple purposes. It is a planning and project management tool that spells out the exact sequence of actions over a given time period while assigning levels of urgency or organizational priority to each. It can also help tell the story of where your digital workplace is headed in terms of changes and enhancements. While you may be fully immersed in your organization's digital transformation trajectory, chances are that most people at your organization are not. The roadmap can be summarized at a high level to communicate progress and assure people across the organization that the changes they are awaiting (hopefully with bated breath) will be rolling out in a timely and logical sequence.

Once you and your collaborators are satisfied with the roadmap and it has been reviewed and approved by all key stakeholders, you will essentially have the green light for moving forward. And if you're already cleared for takeoff, the roadmap will be a great tool for communicating broadly what the digital transformation effort will focus on in the months and years ahead.

Use the guide that follows as a starting point for building a digital roadmap that best suits the scope and complexity of the digital transformation effort, while trying to create something that will be easily understood by those who need to fully understand its implications.

GUIDE TO BUILDING THE DIGITAL TRANSFORMATION ROADMAP

The roadmap should define the exact sequence of activities that you will lead to achieve the desired future state of the digital enterprise. The format of the roadmap is less important. Whether it's a spreadsheet, work plan in a project management tool, slide deck, or combination of these or other formats, the most important thing is that it contains all key pieces of information that will clarify how and when changes will be implemented to those within and outside of the project team.

I recommend building out a roadmap initially that covers 12–24 months, depending on how quickly progress can be made. Depending on how spread out activities are over time, it may be helpful to group activities into two or more phases. This is also useful when there is a bucket of activities for which the timing is yet to be determined. You can simply slot them into a later phase with no specific dates and return to the timing of that phase later on in the project when decisions will be easier.

Here are the key pieces of information you should include in your roadmap. Remember to include *all* activities and milestones that will contribute to project success, not just those related to the technology changes themselves. People- and process-related changes will be just as important, if not more so, in delivering your intended outcomes.

Activity or milestone: These should be specific enough to contain an underlying set of tasks but not so granular as to number in the hundreds. Think of the major steps that will move the effort forward. For example, "Gather CRM system requirements" is an appropriate level of activity for the roadmap, whereas "Meet with CRM system manager" would be a task under this activity better relegated to a more detailed project work plan to be defined and managed by a designated project manager.

For every activity or milestone, include the following key details:

Phase: The phase of the project to which the activity is assigned. For a one- to two-year roadmap, try to limit the number of phases to three or four at most.

Area: Choose the area that this activity or milestone is most closely related to. I use three simple categories: people, process, and technology. *People*-related activities include staffing needs, employee upskilling, engagement of key stakeholders, and many change management approaches that focus on building interest and support across the organization. *Process*-related activities include anything that is focused on process changes and improvements, even if the process is supported by an underlying technology. *Technology*-related activities are those primarily focused on the technology itself, such as reconfiguration of existing tools, technology selection, and system integrations.

Quick win: Put a check mark here if this step is considered a quick win. Quick wins are typically activities that can be conducted relatively rapidly that will lead to noticeable improvements. They are particularly useful early in the digital transformation implementation as a mechanism to leap forward from the current state and build trust and excitement among staff about the additional changes to come. Best candidates for quick wins include pain points, whether process or technology related, that were designated as a priority by those you consulted with during discovery. In other words, these small changes could make a big positive impact on people's ability to get work done.

Status: Use this field as a status tracker for communicating progress along the way. Typical options include not yet started, in progress, and completed.

Start and end dates: The approximate start and end dates of the activity. This provides a more specific time frame of completion within the phase to which the activity or milestone has been assigned.

Challenges addressed: List any challenges from the discovery tracker that will be addressed by this activity. This will be useful for ensuring that all in scope challenges are being addressed while serving as a useful communication tool to reiterate that the issues arising from your discovery work are, in fact, being tended to.

Related systems: List any IT systems from the discovery tracker that relate to the activity or milestone. Again, this will be useful for demonstrating how discovery findings have informed the roadmap and will also help to filter and sort activities by the IT system(s), if any, that they are linked to.

Related opportunities: List any opportunities from the discovery tracker that relate to the activity or milestone. Opportunities hold as much if not more value for the digital transformation effort in that they represent complementary efforts or circumstances that the digital transformation effort can capitalize on. These linkages will reinforce the idea that the digital transformation project is not proceeding in a vacuum, but rather taking the full context of the organization into account.

Dependencies: List any specific dependencies, or activities and conditions that are a prerequisite for completing a given activity or milestone, from the roadmap itself or other related initiatives. This will help with sequencing and assist the team in identifying when roadmap activities are at risk of falling behind due to delays or changes in other related areas.

Your Assignment

- Conduct the Digital Transformation Readiness Assessment, ideally together with your closest project collaborators. As you review the answers, create a plan of action as needed to address any areas where answers did not fall into the "agree" column. You don't need to solve all these issues before proceeding, but they should be top of mind as you proceed down the path of implementation. If left unaddressed for too long, they will come back to bite you later in the journey.

◆ Create the first version of the Digital Transformation Roadmap. This is where the proverbial rubber hits the road, so don't be surprised if you and your collaborators experience a few moments of panic as you contemplate all that you need to accomplish to achieve your stated objectives. If it feels overly ambitions, you're probably on the right track. Phases are your friend here. Map out what is realistic and achievable in phases 1 and 2 and push off the most daunting activities to later phases. At least this gets the ball rolling, and you may find willing champions to ease the burden as you socialize the roadmap with others across the organization. Remember, the path to progress starts with a single step!

CHAPTER 10

Building the Future

All the preparation, planning, stakeholder engagement, and envisioning have led you to this pivotal moment. And you now have a transformation roadmap that will guide the implementation of the first and subsequent rounds of changes to your digital workplace. The work may involve designing, building, and rolling out one or more entirely new systems or giving a light makeover to an existing system. Nevertheless, you will want to make sure that you put end users at the center on every step of the way, designing systems and approaches that not only meet the need but also make your colleagues or constituents jump for joy.

Now it's time to do the hard but highly rewarding work of defining and executing the specific enhancements and changes people have said are most needed. You'll put your product designer hat on while you define user stories and system requirements. This is both an art and a science, so don't worry about getting it perfectly right if you're new to this type of project. You will have a chance to validate and iterate as you go and can team up with subject matter experts along the way.

You'll also need to choose the right technology and partners for the job. Maybe it's evaluating new tools or assessing the capabilities of the technology you already have (or both!). In any case, you'll want to look past the hype (or bad reputations) of the technology you're evaluating to arrive at the very best solution. You'll also consider whether you need to bring in external partners to help develop or roll out the system(s) in question. Just like dating, choosing the right implementation partner can be a tricky decision with significant downstream consequences!

Probably more than any other stage of the transformation process, the implementation phase can be humbling, time-consuming, and disorienting, especially for those undertaking a digital transformation project for the first time. Don't be afraid to ask questions and seek expert advice at every step of the way. Soon you'll be the one to whom others are reaching out for advice.

Define User Stories and Requirements

An important early step when implementing new technology or reconfiguring existing tools is to define detailed user stories and requirements. These will serve as a blueprint for the build process, and as another checkpoint for validating that you are truly meeting the needs of the organization as articulated and prioritized during the discovery and roadmap steps. Whether the implementation is being led internally or will be partially or fully supported by external partners, these specifications will serve as guardrails to keep the end-product true to the future-state vision.

First, some quick definitions.

The practice of collecting *user stories* comes from agile software development. The purpose of user stories is to describe software features from the perspective of the end user to help those selecting or building a system to ensure that they are fully meeting user needs and expectations. The typical format of a user story is as follows:

> As a <user role/persona>, I want to <some action/goal> so that <some benefit/reason>.

Using this simple structure to describe a potential feature, this user-centered methodology defines high-level functionality needs without prescribing a specific solution.

Epics are a collection of user stories that share a broader strategic goal or objective. They are useful for grouping or categorizing user stories and ensuring that groups of user stories are implemented in a way that leads to a clear and usable end-to-end experience for the user.

Requirements are system capabilities needed to solve a user problem or achieve an objective. In other words, what exactly must a technology do to support the end user in achieving the action or goal defined in a user story?

Taken together, user stories, epics, and requirements can build a comprehensive picture of the range of actions and functionalities that a given technology must support. You will then use this information as a guide for selecting the appropriate new or existing technology and, ultimately, building and/or configuring the new or improved system. This user-centered system design approach will ensure that people's needs, not system capabilities, dictate the outcomes of the digital transformation effort.

Utilizing this user story format, you will gather and document all the user stories around the in-scope business process and systems through conversations with end users. First, you'll define a set of *user personas* based on the type of people you will be designing for. User personas are basically categories of user types who will interact with the system in distinct ways. For example, you may have an "accounting specialist" persona to represent staff who are primarily inputting data into the financial management system, while the "finance executive" persona will be primarily concerned with approvals and extracting meaningful reports from the data housed in the system.

Based on the personas you are designing for, you will want to conduct targeted discovery interviews among representatives of each persona type. Remember that these interviews should not revisit ground covered during your initial stakeholder discovery interviews and focus groups but rather uncover detailed needs and workflows related to the specific system and/or business process in question. You might find it useful to review what you heard in the initial discovery rounds from people falling under each persona to determine what additional questions to ask.

Once you have gathered all relevant user stories and assigned them to one or more personas, you will group them into relevant categories or epics. The next step is to think about the *functional requirements* that support each user story. Functional requirements outline what a particular technology must *do* to satisfy the needs of the end user. For example, a user story such as "As a document author, I want to share an editable version of the document with external collaborators so that we can easily work on the document together and retain version control" would translate into the following business requirement:

> A user can securely share a link to the live version of a document with an external collaborator that allows them to edit the document while any changes and comments are recorded and visible to other collaborators.

As you review this rich collection of insights and information, think about the priority level of each user story and requirement. Some prioritizations will be driven by the users themselves. How urgent is their need? How critical a gap will persist if that need goes unmet? The digital transformation project's goals, roadmap, and budget will also need to be considered during prioritization. Perhaps there is an emergent strategic goal that staff don't yet have on their radars but that is deemed critical to achieve in the near future. In these cases, you will have to weigh organizational priorities against end user needs. In many cases, these priorities are aligned. Where they are not, you'll likely want key stakeholders to weigh in on how to balance considerations for the end user experience against strategically important changes to the organization's technology.

You and your collaborators will also need to be creative in thinking about how each epic and/or user story will be addressed. There are typically several ways to satisfy any requirement. Should we use existing technology or leverage a new system? Do we build a custom solution or use off-the-shelf technology? Although there is no formula for making the right decision, this is a good time to review your user stories and requirements with the goals and scope of the digital transformation project in mind.

Finally, before you complete this step, you are encouraged to validate the user stories and requirements with the stakeholders you have included in the process up to this point. By keeping users at the center as you define and refine the problems you are trying to solve, you will ensure that your solutions are tailored to their needs and deliver maximum value.

Selecting the Right Technology

There's no way of getting around it: choosing the right technology is stressful. Products are changing at a dizzying pace, and it's hard for even the savviest tech leader to separate hype from reality. The best solution two or three years ago could now be obsolete. With so much money and so many expectations on the line, you don't want to bet on the wrong horse.

Speaking of horses and betting, any external partners you bring in during this or later stages of your project can be major contributors to the project's ultimate success or failure. Your partner(s) should possess skills and expertise (and time) that are in short supply internally, but they should also be a good culture fit and be able to fully understand, and hold themselves at least partially accountable for, the outcomes you're seeking to achieve.

Take charge of these major decisions with cool, collected precision. Looking back a few months from now, you and others will wonder about how the decisions you made "back then" were so spot-on that they almost seemed clairvoyant!

The technology selection process is more than just demoing tools. When selecting a new, potentially unknown technology solution, you'll need to develop the criteria to be used for identifying and narrowing the field of potential vendors. You'll also want to map out an approach that involves key stakeholders in ways that enhance, rather than derail, the tech selection process and helps you and others avoid being misled by slick sales techniques.

I recommend a two-step selection process that allows you to quickly eliminate technology that doesn't meet the most critical requirements. This allows you to focus more time on deeply understanding how well each plausible candidate stacks up. In many cases, you may be "auditioning" technology that you already have against something new. I'll provide some pointers on how to make an apples-to-apples comparison in these cases and respond to common situations where bias for or against existing tools is standing in the way of a good selection process.

And of course, selection of technology and implementation partners is first and foremost a procurement process. If you're lucky enough to work at an organization that has clear and stringent policies around procurement, don't worry. The approaches outlined are not meant to replace these policies. Rather, they are designed to easily adapt to any procurement approach.

Running a good technology selection process involves clearly documenting everything you are looking for in a top solution and then rating each candidate tool against these set criteria. To narrow the field to only potentially viable candidates, I suggest defining two to five "gating criteria" that are nonnegotiable. Eliminating tools that do not support these essential requirements will save time and heartache as you begin a more granular level of analysis.

In some cases, the rating system you develop may be used alongside any standard systems your organization has in place, such as those that review tools based on the organization's security and compliance standards. Nevertheless, having a detailed analysis that maps to the user stories and requirements your team has defined will not only make the selection process easier, but will also be a tool for clearly explaining to others how you arrived at a particular solution. Once you've narrowed the field to a few top contenders, you can use a demo score sheet that will be filled out by the stakeholders involved in the final selection process. This sheet, which should list the top areas of differentiation between the tools with a standard rating scale, will help those involved to easily understand what they should be paying attention to, thereby placing all reviewers on an equal footing. With this level of rating criteria, I like to provide reviewers with the following options for each major criteria, which are broad enough so as not to be overwhelming but lead to substantive discussions about which solution is best:

- ◆ 1 = Does not meet expectations/unacceptable
- ◆ 2 = Meets expectations/acceptable
- ◆ 3 = Exceeds expectations/outstanding

Selecting the Right Partner

Selecting a vendor to implement a digital solution can be a lot like deciding to get married. You want to make sure you've picked the right partner, one who will be there for you, for better, for worse, and there's a *lot* of money involved. It's important to ask yourself the following five questions before you say, "I do":

1. **Are you a good match? Do your companies align philosophically?**

   As you look for a vendor, particularly in the technology sector, you want to select a reputable company that aligns with your organization's values. Look for a consulting firm that is able to enter into the challenges of implementation with eyes wide open and is committed to your success. They should appreciate that the purpose of the digital transformation project is to more effectively achieve one or more business goals – not just throwing the next shiny new technology over the fence – and as such should be committed to helping you achieve that goal. That means they should be flexible and open to tailoring solutions for your needs rather than simply reusing something they've already built. It also shouldn't be solely about the bottom line for them. A good vendor wants both sides to feel proud about and invested in the project approach and end results.

2. **Can you communicate effectively?**

   There must be open and transparent communication for a project to be successful. Before you select a vendor, make sure your communication styles mesh. For example, if you prefer on-site meetings, are they located nearby? If you want real-time support, are they in your same time zone? How responsive are they over email or chat? Do they speak your "language," as in, do they understand your industry and industry-specific jargon? Prior experience in your industry can be a huge asset because the vendor will already be familiar with industry terminology and typical system needs. Request a getting-acquainted meeting during the selection process, which you facilitate, so you can see firsthand how they interact with your team in more of a roll-up-your-sleeves tactical meeting. You may be surprised at how many seemingly good vendors begin showing a different face once they step away from their cookie-cutter presentation comfort zone.

3. **Is there good culture alignment?**

You should be confident that your vendor values active listening and honest, transparent communication. You need to be able to clearly explain your needs and wants (and they need to really listen) to implement a solution that meets your needs. If the potential partner is a software vendor or designated partner, they should be forthcoming about what functionality is available now versus under development. And if something is under development, they should be able to provide a clear time frame for its deployment. They should also feel comfortable sharing their candid perspectives and expertise gained from previous, similar engagements, even if this causes them to lose additional business. For example, your vendor could help you reconsider costly customizations if they are able to support the need through creative use of out-of-the-box functionality. Healthy communication will create a safe space for that push-and-pull dynamic. The vendor's approach to the procurement process and negotiation, as well as information from previous customers, will give you further insight into their work style and help you determine if it's a good match.

4. **Are they right-sized for your organization? Do their skills complement your internal team?**

Consider if the vendor is sized right for your organization and if they complement your in-house skills. Giant consulting firms with 10,000-plus staff can offer a sense of security because they are financially stable and have a lot of customers and broad experience. You can be reasonably confident that they will be around for years to come, which could be an asset if you're looking for a long-term partner. However, they may not be as nimble and specialized as smaller firms that focus on a particular industry or sector. Smaller firms usually have consultants with more years of experience and specific industry expertise, and typically have lower overhead. A local firm could be a better choice if you value in-person support.

Most importantly, consultants should complement your staff without duplicating or competing with internal expertise.

Consider your in-house resources (both skillset and availability) when selecting a consulting partner. Does the consulting firm fill the right gaps while freeing up internal resources to do what they do best while growing professionally from observing the consultants in action? You want to make sure that the vendor brings the right balance of stability, agility, and skills, while being willing and able to transfer their knowledge to the internal resources who will ensure the long-term success of this initiative.

5. **Do they have relevant project experience and a good track record?**

   Find out about a vendor's track record by talking with their current and past customers and asking about their strengths and weaknesses. Potential vendors will share references, but couple that with your own due diligence to get a balanced view. Be sure to reach out to industry peers as well – their projects are likely relevant to your own goals. You should also consider how long they have been in business, if they're growing or downsizing, and if they have relevant certifications for your digital solutions. A positive track record and a sense of how projects went after their involvement will give you confidence going into your own project.

6. **Are they transparent about total costs?**

   Organizations must be prudent about digital investments and understand the total cost of implementation. Some vendors may offer a lower upfront price, but there are costly add-on services or hidden costs such as "premium" support that you're going to need. How is ongoing support billed? You'll need clarity on the total cost up front so you can make an informed decision. However, price should not be the only deciding factor. Consider the cost of not trusting your vendor or having your implementation go sideways. Be sure to ask about their processes to ensure projects stay on budget and on schedule. An exceptional vendor will help you be mindful of cost creep at every step because they want both parties to succeed.

Launching the Implementation Process

The time to kick-start your organization's digital transformation journey has arrived. Although you and the people you've assembled might be ready to jump right in, it's important not to overlook the crucial step of officially launching the implementation process. Take the time to announce to staff that implementation of planned changes is under way. Whether an email, a blog post, or a "brown-bag" lunch-and-learn event, consider how big or little you want this launch to feel. Regardless of which communication channel(s) you choose, this launch should communicate that the digital transformation project implementation phase is officially under way and that it will be transparent, collaborative, and inclusive.

As you craft the messaging and approach around the project launch, think about the ways in which your audiences might respond. Their responses might be influenced by the messaging itself but also by the person or persons who will deliver the message. Should the CEO or other key leader be the messenger, or should another member of the project team? Or perhaps a joint statement from the effort's steering group? This will largely depend on your organization's culture and what you think will be the most strategic and effective way of transmitting the information.

Regardless of the messenger, this is an opportunity to emphasize the strategic importance of the digital transformation project, its tie-ins to other projects or initiatives, and any other contextual information that will make the project more relatable to staff. To help with this, consider sharing excerpts from the discovery research, digital transformation roadmap, or other key outputs to emphasize how much listening and thought have already gone into the planning process. Do not let any project-related communication go out without a genuine request for staff questions and feedback. People may not take you up on it right away, but as you continue to emphasize this type of "open door" policy, they will take notice and hopefully seize the opportunity to weigh in.

Managing the Implementation Process

Up until this point, your planning process has been largely centered around establishing a shared vision for the future. The development of the digital transformation roadmap is where strategy turned to tactics. Now, a layer down from the roadmap's activities and milestones, what exactly needs to be done to implement the envisioned changes in a timely and impactful manner?

If you're a seasoned project manager, this type of project planning may be second nature. It involves identifying all the tasks to be performed under each major activity in the roadmap, who's responsible, and by when. If this type of project planning isn't in your wheelhouse, it may take some adjustment and several iterations to get it right. The first consideration is what project management style you will use to organize the implementation process.

Project management for technology deployments typically follows one of two styles, waterfall or agile. Waterfall is a more traditional, sequential project management approach that involves a lot of up-front planning. It works best for projects where requirements are determined and fixed. In this method you establish your main activities and their subcomponents and lay them out in a sequence. Waterfall projects are typically tracked through Gantt charts, a bar chart that lays out tasks over time, as shown in Figure 10.1.

Agile is an alternate project management approach that best supports iterative product development cycles and prioritizes collaboration and continuous feedback. This approach works best for complex technology projects where all of the requirements are not fully defined up front. *Scrum*, one of the most popular agile methodologies, organizes user stories into one- to three-week product development "sprints"

Task	Lead	% Complete	1	2	3	4	5	6	7	8	9	10
Stakeholder Discovery												
Project Strategy & Metrics	Jasmine	100%	■									
Change Mgmt. & Communication Planning	Chen	100%		■								
User Mapping	Arjun	80%			■							
Create List of Interviewees	Jasmine	40%				■						
Conduct Interviews	Chen	0%					■					
Baseline Survey	Arjun	0%					■					
Platform Evaluation & Selection												
Develop Assessment Criteria	Jasmine	0%						■				
Conduct Landscape Analysis	Amrita	0%							■			
Evaluate Selected Platforms	Joyann	0%								■		
Platform Selection	Em	0%										■

Figure 10.1 Typical waterfall project plan in Gantt chart format.

where work is defined, tracked, and rolled out in batches. With daily team standup meetings, usually lasting 15 minutes, and end-of-sprint reviews, constant communication and progress tracking are baked into the process. Agile projects can be tracked using a Kanban visualization (Figure 10.2) where tasks are typically organized into three or more columns according to their current status, such as "To Do," "In Progress," and "Done." Project participants typically track and update tasks themselves so that the project manager and their fellow collaborators can quickly see the status of all work in progress forming part of that sprint.

I recommend taking a hybrid approach to project management for digital transformation project implementation. Start with a waterfall project plan for the overall project trajectory and then break down multiple build-and-test cycles into agile work cycles or "sprints" of one to two weeks each. This approach supports the implementation team to stick to an overarching plan and timeline but allows for a moderate degree of iterative product development and collaborative work planning among all team members.

The overall project implementation plan is typically depicted as a Gantt- or waterfall-style work plan. The waterfall format supports succinct communication of tasks, timelines, and the people responsible for each task who will take the project to the finish line. Its strength lies in the ability to show a bird's-eye view of plans and progress over a relatively long period of time, such as a year or more, while the agile Kanban view typically shows just one sprint at a time. The waterfall plan can easily be extracted from the transformation

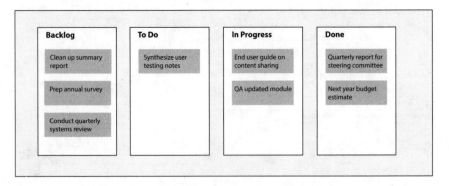

Figure 10.2   Typical agile project plan in Kanban format.

roadmap while providing a greater level of detail regarding the tasks and assignments under each activity.

You may already have one or more project management tools in place that will be a perfect fit for managing an agile and/or waterfall-style project plan. Many popular project management solutions allow you to easily toggle between these different work plan styles. Whatever style and tool you choose, you'll want to validate the plan with stakeholders and ensure that you've sufficiently accounted for people's available hours, holidays, and other planned outages or interruptions. And as with any good plan, it should be maintained as a "living" document, adjusted as you go to reflect the current realities of project execution.

Designing a Great User Experience

The practice of user experience (UX) design has experienced a meteoric rise in popularity over the last few decades. Before Apple and Steve Jobs came along, it was rare to think about technology and design in the same breath. But once consumers began realizing how a functional, user-centered design could convert a confusing or alienating technology, product, or application into an inviting and pleasing experience, a new era began.

UX design is an aspect of product design focused on how people interact with a digital tool. This includes physical interactions (clicking, scrolling, tapping), user flow, and how users feel throughout the experience.

According to the World Design Organization, UX design is:[1]

"the process design teams use to create products that provide meaningful and relevant experiences to users. This involves the design of the entire process of acquiring and integrating the product, including aspects of branding, design, usability and function."

So what does this mean for digital transformation?

At one level, any application or digital tool you are counting on people to use frequently in the course of their work should be inviting and pleasing to the end user. That may sound simplistic, but a lot goes into making a piece of technology inviting and pleasing. Think of products like the iPhone or iPad and the countless hours involved in every new iteration of that combination of hardware and software. It feels simple, at best almost effortless. But the process of arriving at that level of simplicity and user-friendliness is far from simple.

Not every digital transformation leader will magically transform into a pro UX designer or Steve Jobs. But many useful principles and practices from the world of UX design can be incorporated into the process of selecting and rolling out new digital tools, or reconfiguring the ones you already have.

If you use any popular consumer mobile apps or websites, you've been taking part in an ongoing UX design experiment, whether you know it or not. In essence, UX design is about making technology more accessible and useful (and in some cases, more addictive!) based on observations of human interaction with a technology product. UX designers observe human behaviors and then modify a product based on what they think will best achieve the desired result, whether that's the number of clicks, amount of time spent browsing, or other metrics of importance.

This is yet another moment during the digital transformation project that provides you an opportunity to wear a different hat – this time, that of a UX designer. What's required? Empathy (again!), keen observation, and a sense of what constitutes a pleasing interaction with an otherwise cold and potentially alienating piece of technology. Don't worry, it's not as hard as it sounds. We all have a designer living inside of us, and if you need some assistance at any point along the way, there are many knowledgeable people and helpful resources out there that you can call upon.

Think of the systems and applications you interact with every day, both for work and personal use. Are there certain aspects of your experience as a user that are frustrating, delightful, intuitive, or depressing? UX design is a set of methods that can help people feel a certain way about their interaction with a particular technology. Unfortunately, for much of the technology we interact with at work, we may feel like the UX designer was on an indefinite sabbatical. This trend stops with you. Say it with me: "From here forward, good UX design will be a guiding principle for the systems we select, design, and deploy."

Your mission for this part of the journey is to familiarize yourself with the theory and practice of UX design. Even if you're not planning to do any customization of existing or new systems as far as UX is concerned, it's still enormously helpful for at least some members of the digital transformation project team to be conversant in UX design. It is, to a large degree, what will drive the usability and user likes and dislikes of different systems, so it's important to anticipate, and plan for, the aspects of enterprise technology that will surprise and delight users, and those that will cause them unnecessary levels of frustration.

Your Assignment

◆ If your digital transformation effort calls for changes to existing systems or selection of new systems, begin the process of cataloging user stories and requirements. A spreadsheet or similar format can be used for this and will convert easily into a build plan once you're ready to begin that work. The best way to gather this information is to sit down with current or prospective end users and walk through with them the things that they need to be able to do with said system. Think ahead about the different personas you envision interacting with the system, and select participants who can serve as representatives of each persona type.

At the outset of these discussion, you'll want to familiarize those you're speaking to with the overarching objectives of the project and the specific challenges to be solved. If they're not already familiar with the concept of user stories, a brief introduction will be useful. This will help frame the discussion and make it easier for them to communicate their needs in a form that you can easily translate into functional requirements.

(Continued)

(Continued)

Once you have a critical mass of user stories, start grouping them into logical epics that reflect core groups of functionality. Then you can begin defining the system's functional requirements that will support each epic. If you will be working with a vendor to support the system selection or build, this upfront work will be hugely helpful in jump-starting that process and will help make sure the vendor is entering the project with a full sense of what is required. This can also be useful information to include in an RFP during the vendor selection process, and will help weed out any vendors that are not equipped, or interested, in approaching the project in the way that you and your stakeholders envision.

Don't let perfect be the enemy of good at this stage. There will be ample time to refine and adjust the requirements as you learn more. This step will simply get you closer to building a system that ultimately delivers on the promises of the digital transformation effort by more clearly communicating, and validating, what is to be achieved.

♦ Within your project team, hold one or more discussion about UX design and the design principles that are most important to the people you have heard from during the project so far. If time allows, it might be useful to read a few current articles or scan a few books available to gather valuable perspectives that will serve you in subsequent stages of the project.

CHAPTER 11

Introducing Change

"When the winds of change blow, some people build walls and others build windmills."

– Chinese proverb

Think of change management, or as I prefer to say, change facilitation, as the beating heart of your digital transformation journey. It is the one thing, aside from the technology itself, that will determine whether your efforts succeed or fail.

A well-executed approach to facilitating change supports short-term adoption of new ways of working while ensuring the longevity and continued relevance of new tools and approaches. And although most literature about change management emphasizes the importance of leadership support, this alone will not carry the day. Change champions are needed at all levels for transformational change to "stick."

Managing change effectively is not a once and done activity, despite often being characterized this way. It is a continuous set of considerations and actions, starting from the earliest stages of a transformation effort and continuing well past "rollout." It is also cyclical in nature. Once one change cycle ends, another one begins (and on and on we go!).

Here's where it helps to play armchair psychologist – or even anthropologist. People are complex beings who bring their varied histories and experiences to the workplace, along with a healthy dose of personality. Everett Rogers (1931–2004), an American sociologist, is credited with coining the phrase "early adopter" in his landmark text, *Diffusion of Innovations*, published in 1962. The book went on to become essential reading for professionals from a variety of disciplines, ranging from marketing and communications to public health, concerned with driving certain types of behavior change among groups and even entire societies.

Rogers's basic premise is that groups of people adopt innovations according to predictable patterns, regardless of the population or innovation in question. By understanding these patterns, those looking to introduce something new into the population can use targeted approaches that work with, rather than against, people's natural orientation toward change. For the purposes of designing a suitable change management approach for the digital transformation project, it's useful to think about where the majority of employees at your organization might fall within the Rogers diffusion of innovations curve (see Figure 11.1), whether this distribution differs from the norm, and how you can shape your adoption strategy accordingly.

The other key thing to consider are the characteristics of an innovation that drive decisions and behaviors around adoption. Rogers outlines five characteristics (see Figure 11.2) that people generally look at when evaluating an innovation.[1] From a technology adoption standpoint, it will be important to craft specific "appeals" or talking points for each adopter category that address these five characteristics.

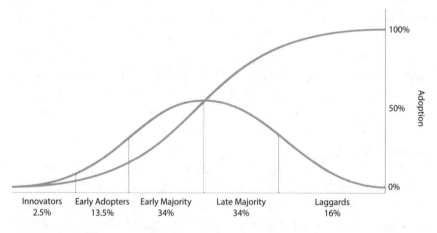

Figure 11.1   Diffusion of innovations curve from the work of Everett Rogers.

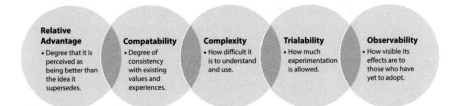

Relative Advantage	Compatability	Complexity	Trialability	Observability
• Degree that it is perceived as being better than the idea it supersedes.	• Degree of consistency with existing values and experiences.	• How difficult it is to understand and use.	• How much experimentation is allowed.	• How visible its effects are to those who have yet to adopt.

Figure 11.2   Five innovation characteristics that drive adoption from the work of Everett Rogers.

What does this all mean for you as a digital transformation leader? In short, it means that you cannot alter people's prewired orientation to change. What you can control is how the change is seen and understood, especially by those who have the biggest aversion to change. For instance, how well it aligns with individual or organizational values and goals, and how it is "worth the trouble" of experiencing a few bumps in the road to reach what's on the other side.

Table 11.1 outlines suggested appeals or messages for each adopter type aimed at dissipating any resistance they might have to adoption of new technologies and ways of working. Remember that while messaging from the team rolling out the changes can be effective among the most willing adopter types (i.e. Innovators, Early Adopters, and Early Majority), communication directly from peers and other trusted colleagues becomes more important as you go across the curve and is critical for driving adoption among people in the Late Majority and Laggard categories.

The bottom line is that everyone has different levels of comfort with change, and that's okay and expected. As a digital transformation leader, be empathetic to your people's different orientations toward change by meeting them where they are and supporting them to comfortably adopt to new ways of working at a scale and pace that feels comfortable to them.

Communicating About Change

As you begin to think about rolling out the changes being planned as part of the digital transformation project, you'll need to craft the right language to get people to join you on the path to progress. It's safe to

Table 11.1 Dominant characteristics of the five adopter types and suggested appeals to drive change.

Adopter type Percentage of typical population	Dominant characteristics and values	Suggested appeals
Innovators 2.5%	**Venturesome,** expanded and diverse social networks, drawn to other innovators, access to resources, fast learners, ability to grasp complex information, ability to cope with high degree of uncertainty, willing to accept setbacks, may not be respected by other members of a local system, **gatekeeper of new ideas into a system and thus crucial to adoption**	• Changes reflect state-of-the-art, best in class capabilities and work approaches. • You will be among first to try/test the solution. • We need your help shaping the way we use new tools and approaches to make them useful to others.
Early adopters 13.5%	**Respected,** more integrated into local system than innovators, more likely than other types to be opinion leaders, change agents, role models, **decreases uncertainty about a new idea by adopting it and sharing a subjective evaluation with near-peers**	• [From senior leader] Changes are being introduced for the benefit of the organization and your specific department. • Several features will help you work more efficiently. • We need your help to introduce new ways of working. • Your feedback will help tailor/improve the experience for others.
Early majority 34%	**Deliberate,** interact frequently with peers, rarely opinion leaders, numerous (usually one-third of a population), longer decision process, **provide interconnectedness in the local system**	• [From senior leader] Many of your colleagues/peers are beginning to see the benefits of these new tools and approaches. • Features that you might find particularly useful include.... • These changes will support the organization and the work of your department in the following ways....

Adoption typically reaches critical mass or the "tipping point" when the majority of people in the preceding three groups have adopted an innovation.

Late majority 34%	Skeptical, adoption often due to pressure from peers, skeptical and cautious, *most uncertainty needs to be removed before they feel it's safe to adopt*	• [From senior leader] These new ways of working will . . . [state personal benefits] • X% of people have already adopted these changes. • View these case studies that showcase examples/testimonials of how people are already benefiting. • Read these tips on how to get the most from these changes.
Laggards 16%	**Traditional**, isolated in social networks, gravitate toward others with traditional values, suspicious of innovations and change agents, lengthy decision process long after they become aware of new idea, **want to be certain of an innovation's success before adopting**	• [From senior leader] These new ways of working have already benefited employees in the following ways . . . [include statistics if available] • Ways we continue to enhance the value of these changes for every employee include . . . . • Learn more about how [colleague names] are realizing the following benefits . . . .

Adapted from Everett Rogers, *Diffusion of Innovations*, 4th ed., 1995.

assume that not everyone has a clear definition of digital transformation floating around in their heads. You'll also want to begin crafting talking points that you can use to effectively and confidently communicate about key aspects of the project and what to expect. Armed with these essential tools, you'll be ready to forge ahead.

How you communicate about digital transformation could be the deciding factor in the effort's ultimate success. We're not all naturally gifted communicators, but there are plenty of proven practices that you can use to guide this aspect of the work. Earlier in this book, you had the opportunity to explore your leadership strengths and areas for improvement. If communication is not your greatest strength, enlist the support of the best communicators you know, within and outside of work, to get this part right. Once you have the right definition and talking points to describe what the digital transformation effort is about and why people should embrace it, the rest should come easily.

The steps introduced in the following section will give you a solid starting point for crafting your own language around digital transformation. This language will change over time as you converse and collaborate with others, so do not let perfect be the enemy of the good. For now, it's sufficient to have language that you feel comfortable with and that resonates with your intended audiences. Once you've drafted some of this language, it may be a good idea to test it out on those you trust to give you honest feedback, so you can be ready for all the important discussions you'll be having along the way.

My advice to you at this stage is the following: know that if your eventual goal is to honor and amplify the contributions of the people who will ultimately benefit from the outcomes of this project, you can do no wrong. Be humble, learn more than you thought possible, admit when you are off track, and enjoy the process of becoming an even more capable leader.

Change Communication Explained

As humans, we resist change. It's in our nature to seek comfort and security. Any disruption to our way of doing or being can be scary or even threatening. According to Gartner, 73% of change-affected employees report experiencing high to moderate stress levels.[2]

As a digital transformation leader, how do you make sure staff understand the upcoming changes while reducing their anxiety? You meet people where they are, providing right-sized information at every step of the way.

Change communication consists of the messages and channels used to convey information to all who will be impacted. Audiences can include people within and outside of your organization, depending on who will ultimately be affected.

Notably, few organizations communicate change well. According to the 2019 Edelman Trust Barometer, only 38% of employees who have experienced workplace transformation say that their employer communicated effectively about the changes, and only 36% say their employers were honest about changes employees would face.[3]

Since people tend to resist anything that disrupts the status quo, the goal of change communication is to get ahead of this resistance. Sending the right message to the right people at the right time throughout the transformation effort helps bring people along and feel some sense of control.

Change communication can be used to:

- Build awareness of the reasons for change and how staff will benefit
- Provide forums for people to share their views and concerns
- Build trust in the organization's ability to carry out the change successfully

(Continued)

(Continued)

♦ Provide staff with an opportunity to guide how the change will affect them, both as professionals and as human beings

Tips for Effectively Communicating Change

Here are some things to keep in mind as you communicate with employees and other key stakeholders before, during, and after your digital transformation project.

Keep talking. The mantra "communicate early and often" is especially important when communicating about change. People fear the unknown. Share a steady flow of information about your project every step of the way. If it feels like you are overcommunicating, you are probably doing it right.

Make leaders visible at the beginning. When it comes to workplace transformation, employees want to hear from leadership, at least at the very start. It's reassuring to know that leaders are aligned with the goals of the effort and that they are committed to its success. This will reinforce that it's not something that can be ignored. Exercise caution around making leaders the only spokespeople, as this will likely contribute to feelings that this is a top-down effort, a perception that can increase resistance to change. Once leaders have had their say, it's time for people at all levels of the organization to become active and vocal participants in the exciting process under way.

Develop targeted, customizable messaging. As Everett Rogers teaches us, only a small proportion of people in an organization are typically early adopters of change. Others will be skeptical from the get-go. Most will fall somewhere in between. You will need to clearly articulate to all of them the value and impact of the project in a way that they will hear and understand. Start by coming up with a set of core messages that explain the whys of your transformation effort.

Then make sure your communications plan addresses the top questions employees will want answered during this process.

Share a vision for the future. Perhaps the most important question employees want answered is "What does this mean for me?" This is often referred to as the "what's in it for me" question, or WIIFM. One way to get the ball rolling is by introducing a clear and simple vision of what the future-state of the organization will look like post-transformation. All other communications should build on this vision, helping connect the dots for those who will be affected.

Meet people where they are. Keep language simple and choose a medium that matches your message. Most people prefer face-to-face communication when it comes to hearing about change. Virtual or in-person town halls, team meetings, short videos, and webinars are all great ways to convey news about your transformation. Reserve email and internal news posts for brief updates and announcements.

Listen, listen, listen. Provide plenty of opportunities for employees to share what they want, need, and expect from an improved digital workplace. Ask for feedback. Host small group listening sessions. Set up forms or an email address for people to submit their thoughts and questions. Make sure you address any questions either directly or in future communications. A rolling list of related Q&As in an accessible location is good for this.

Engage managers. Digital transformation projects can take a long time to produce visible benefits. How do you keep everyone excited and engaged while the work is progressing? Lean on managers and change champions who are well informed and enthusiastic about what's to come. Managers are seen as trusted sources of information and can help to dispel any myths or misconceptions floating around. Make sure they have all the latest information on project progress and what it means for their direct reports and the organization.

(Continued)

(Continued)

Celebrate success. Throw a launch party to celebrate new ways of working with the entire organization. Find fun ways for people to learn about and use the new tools and processes to help them immediately see some of the benefits. The funny thing about change is, while we fear it, we also love it when it delivers on the promise of something better. So let people enjoy, explore, and show their appreciation for everyone who worked tirelessly to bring the future-state vision to life.

Bring on the reviews. Some people will love the changes. Some people will not. You cannot please everyone, but you can quickly sense if the changes are being well received. Encourage people to let you know how they feel about the transformation. Lean on some of the tactics you used to gather feedback throughout the process so you can discern any discontent. Perhaps send out an anonymous survey a few weeks post-launch to get a read, once people have had time to digest and explore.

Iterate and evolve. Once you have celebrated and the glow of launch has worn off, it's time to dive right on back in and make things even better. The pace of technology waits for no one. There will always be user feedback to address, more processes to improve, and enhancements to make. Continue to communicate with and listen to your colleagues and find ways to make things better. This will support the continuous improvement of your tools and processes and will build staff confidence over time that the future is indeed bright.

Preparing for Launch

The moment has come. You've been hard at work for months, if not years, to implement the planned changes and it's almost time to roll them out to the entire organization. It's natural at this stage to be tempted to rush through the final steps leading up to the launch.

Please do not. Although it does not require a huge lift to get the launch "right," a little thoughtfulness and creativity at this stage, when the project team is likely exhausted, will go a long way.

The theme for this stage of the project is to go beyond conventional. This applies to how you provide training and support as well as how you launch and promote what's new. It's helpful to think of the enhanced or entirely new systems and processes you'll be rolling out as a new product. You'll be playing the role of product marketer. Sound like fun?

Think about the old saying that goes something like "If a tree falls in the forest and no one hears it . . ." Well, the same principle applies to the launch and promotion of new tools and ways of working. If no one hears about it, did it really happen? Most of us are not natural promoters, especially those of us who tend to lead digital transformation efforts. So don't be surprised or discouraged if you're feeling like a fish out of water during this pivotal yet late step in the process.

By now, you and your collaborators have likely been sharing the expected benefits of the project in so many ways, shapes, and forms that it seems impossible that anyone could not know or be excited about what's on the horizon. But you'd be wrong. People are bombarded with so much information in the course of the workday that it's often surprising how little gets absorbed. For the purposes of your launch promotion plan, assume the worst: that very few in the organization know about the exciting new capabilities and benefits that they are about to experience as a result of this project.

Once that assumption is set, you have a green field of planning and execution before you. Be loud and proud. Operate as if this is the first time anyone has heard the words "digital" and "transformation" in combination with each other. In so doing, you will be sure to inspire sufficient levels of interest and excitement that will lead to widespread adoption across the organization.

Use the following Launch Plan outline to plot the way forward. Communication – the tone, tenor, and mode of delivery – will matter more than ever at this late stage, so think through every message and action carefully. Now is also the time to rally your key stakeholders, champions, and other supportive and influential voices in support of the cause.

Launch Communications and Promotion Plan Template

Use this template to plan the launch and ongoing promotion of new tools and ways of working to be introduced through the digital transformation effort. Thoughtful attention to detail during this step will help ensure maximum awareness and adoption of the changes you are introducing.

Part 1: Introduction

Provide an overview of the digital transformation initiative including the core challenge(s), the transformation effort being undertaken to address the challenge, and how this communications and promotion plan will support your audiences through this change. Be sure to detail here any relevant goals and objectives that you aim to achieve through this plan.

Pre-launch communication campaign

Activity	Timing	Audience	Channel/ Medium	Key messages

Part 2: Pre-Launch Communication

Provide a brief summary of the pre-launch campaign and how it will support your change effort. Then document the tactical approach for these communications, including target audience, medium, key messages, timing, and any related materials that will be developed.

Pre-launch marketing materials

Material	Timing	Owner/Creator	Medium	Key messages

Part 3: Launch Activities and Communications

When rolling out new initiatives, tools, processes, and so on, it's important to have a moment in time for staff to coalesce around and celebrate the change. Often, launch day will involve an activity or event to bring everyone together and promote buy-in across the organization, as well as more logistical communications to lay out any immediate changes. Use this section to detail the "run of show" for launch day, including all events, messages, materials, swag, and the like.

Launch materials

Activity	Timing	Activity type (event, message, etc.)	Audience	Related materials

Part 4: Post-Launch Adoption Support

In this section, you will provide a tactical approach for guiding adoption of the changes across the organization or the subset of the organization that is the focus of this effort. This may include incentives like contests (e.g. a scavenger hunt), communications campaigns to share tips and guidance, ongoing opportunities for training and support, and any other creative ideas the team can come up with.

Post-launch materials

Activity	Timing	Activity type (event, message, etc.)	Audience	Related materials

Part 5: Measuring Success

You may also want to consider how you will measure the success of the communications and promotion activities. This may include any analytics around how many were reached and actually engaged in the various events and communications.

Your Assignment

- ◆ Referring back to Table 11.1, begin crafting messaging or appeals that will speak to people across the organization at different points along the diffusion of innovations curve. As you do this, refer to the section "Change Communication Explained" for best practices on crafting messages that will resonate with your different audiences and adopter types.
- ◆ Use the templates provided to develop your launch plan. Be as creative (and, dare I say it, fun) as possible with this plan. Now is the time to celebrate and everyone is invited to the party. If marketing, promotion, and party planning are not your forte, enlist the help of the others who will relish this rare opportunity to show off their skills in this area.

CHAPTER 12

Stewarding the Digital Workplace

Your hard work and collaborative approach have paid off and you are now basking in the glow of a successful launch. While things may be running smoothly, don't count on this tranquility lasting long. Organizations are dynamic environments with constantly changing priorities and needs. So are people. And the technology that you implement today is not static. Cloud applications are in a constant state of evolution, often changing significantly with every new release or update.

Enter the concept of digital workplace governance, or what I prefer to call digital workplace stewardship. The concept is simple. As someone responsible for the state of digital technology at your organization, you'll find that it's good practice to keep an eye on things. It's even better to put in place practices and standards that support the continuous improvement of your digital tools to monitor and maintain their relevance, performance, and usability.

In this chapter, I'll introduce you to some simple and highly effective methods and tools for practicing exemplary digital workplace stewardship. This is just like maintaining a car: it's best to start when that car is new instead of waiting until it falls apart. Although you may be tempted to put off this task until the first signs of trouble, I urge you to get started right away. The foundations you put in place now will ensure your readiness for the winding road ahead.

Governance Considerations

Tending to the health of your digital workplace is an ongoing task. Enterprise technology, just like cars, will suffer from the neglect of its owners or stewards. The plan you will develop in this step will serve as a clear, right-sized approach to maintaining the integrity and usefulness of the collection of tools you have worked so hard to intentionally select, design, and deploy.

In many ways, your approach to digital workplace governance is an extension of the digital transformation project itself. This is another job that you simply cannot do alone. And you'll likely want to involve some of the same champions and other key stakeholders that you engaged with during earlier stages of the project.

Most of all, this step is about resilience. Once you have a governance plan in place, your digital workplace will be well positioned to weather any storm.

The biggest challenge when it comes to the governance of your digital workplace is developing a right-sized set of approaches that are well matched to your technology landscape and available resources. If the governance approach is too elaborate and time-consuming, it will likely end up on the garbage heap of failed initiatives. Too lightweight, and the digital enterprise will soon slide back into the exact type of chaos you worked so hard to eliminate.

Use the Digital Workplace Stewardship Plan template in the following section to help you develop a clear strategy for tackling this important, ongoing work and identify the people who will support it.

The first consideration is roles and responsibilities. In general, you will have at least three groups bearing some of the responsibilities for digital workplace stewardship. First is what I call the digital workplace leadership team. This may or may not be the same group of people responsible for leading the digital transformation project. Regardless of who sits on this team, they should have the ability to develop and lead or sponsor both strategic and tactical types of activity to ensure that your enterprise tech stack continues to serve the organization as intended and expected.

Next, you will ideally have a group of digital workplace champions. These could be some or all of the same people you enlisted as change champions to support the rollout of the digital transformation project, but think this through carefully. What you're looking for in this group is to serve as your eyes and ears regarding how technology is performing in the organization. If people see you as responsible for the changes that they are unhappy with, you will be the last to know about them. Your champions can keep you informed about any trouble brewing so you can address it before it becomes a full-blown crisis.

And then there's the support team. These are generally people on the IT team who are providing end-user support to system users. They will likely also include any IT system administrators, non-IT system owners, and IT consultants.

The next set of considerations is related to the routine approaches you will be implementing in service to digital workplace governance: strategic decision-making, risk management, and continuous improvement. Strategic decision-making activities are focused on ensuring the ongoing relevance and alignment of digital workplace tools to the strategic objectives of the business units that use them and to the organization as a whole. When there are major shifts in organizational strategies or structures, governance can ensure that the role technology plays to support the organization's stated goals is thought about alongside other typical considerations such as resourcing and internal communications.

Risk management in the context of digital workplace governance has to do with proactively identifying and addressing potential risks to system performance and adoption. It is not uncommon to see technology adoption take a nosedive shortly after an initially successful launch. Many times, this is due to a lack of adequate support for end users as they try to use the system to perform increasingly complex sets of tasks. It can also result from confusion or incomplete understanding among end users about how or when to use a certain technology. Over time, confusion can increase as new tools, some of which may be unsanctioned, are introduced into the workplace. Like with most types of risks, it is important to get ahead of these risks before they become widespread and irreversible.

Finally, the plan you create should outline an approach to the continuous improvement of the digital workplace. In the next chapter, you will have a chance to operationalize this aspect of your plan by defining the key metrics you wish to track. For now, this is a chance to be thoughtful about how a combination of system-generated data, end-user feedback, and other observed performance measures can help you to communicate the success of these tools while also detecting when it's time to take action.

Governance Approaches

The primary goal of digital workplace governance is to maintain the integrity and relevance of IT systems in light of the organization's evolving priorities and work styles. It is recommended that the organization take a lightweight, shared approach to system governance that is primarily focused on **strategic decision-making, risk management,** and **continuous improvement.** Following are recommendations on these three areas of activity.

STRATEGIC DECISION-MAKING

The digital workplace should fully support and be in alignment with the strategic goals of the organization. **Through routinely reviewing system metrics and engaging in conversations with key stakeholders, digital workplace stewards should regularly validate the current digital workplace strategy and identify any gaps or weaknesses.** When major changes to organizational priorities or workstreams occur, stewards should reassess the function of the digital workplace in light of those changes while thinking proactively about the role of technology in supporting implementation and rollout of any anticipated organizational changes.

RISK MANAGEMENT

Once the initial hurdle of organization-wide adoption of new or reconfigured tools is cleared, the largest risk to the digital workplace is that end users begin to feel their digital tools are not adequately supporting their work processes. The second largest risk is that users perceive their digital tools as not being well supported or maintained by the organization. Both scenarios can drive users away from officially sanctioned tools and lead them to adopt often disruptive and less secure "shadow" IT systems.

The IT department or team can engage in several activities to mitigate these risks. First and foremost, they should stay on top of and proactively manage all IT system updates. For most tools, this involves staying apprised of upcoming system changes and then following a consistent change management process (see Addendum B for suggested change management steps) when new features or system changes are expected to have a noticeable effect on the end-user experience.

How responses to user support requests are handled is equally critical. Rapid IT response times send a message to end users that they have full support to make the best use of their digital tools. **The IT help desk or support team should endeavor not only to troubleshoot user issues but also to treat every user interaction as an opportunity to check in on their overall level of comfort with their digital tools. When appropriate, they should proactively offer ad hoc or more structured training based on a user's specific needs.**

IT help desk tickets are an important source of data on IT response times, frequency of recurring issues, areas where more user training may be needed, and desired system enhancements. IT support staff should ensure that this data is routinely analyzed and reported out for use in decision-making by the digital workplace stewards.

It is also recommended that IT support staff, together with designated digital workplace or digital transformation champions, deliver regular, targeted user communication, learning content, and ad hoc user tutorials that demonstrate how new or existing digital tools can add value in the context of each department's work. Finally, end users should always feel that they are being heard and responded to regarding any questions or concerns they have around the digital workplace. Champions and IT support staff should work closely together to maintain two-way, open, transparent channels of communication about all matters related to the digital workplace.

CONTINUOUS IMPROVEMENT

Digital workplace performance should be routinely assessed and reviewed in accordance with a Digital Workplace Measurement and Reporting Guide (see Chapter 13). **In addition to key metrics collected from the IT systems themselves and periodic user surveys, IT support staff or other designated individuals should**

be regularly soliciting and recording user feedback on desired system changes and enhancements.

It is neither feasible nor desirable to implement all requests from users. However, this pipeline or backlog of user requests can serve as an important guideline for digital workplace stewards as they plan and budget for system enhancements during each budget cycle. Best practice for maintaining a system enhancement backlog involves the collection of user stories (i.e. details on what the user would like to be able to do with the system, not just a feature or piece of functionality) and a relative prioritization of these user stories based on their level of urgency, cost and complexity to implement, and volume of users that would stand to benefit.

Once system changes and enhancements are prioritized based on user needs, they should then be passed on to the digital workplace stewards for planning purposes. The stewards should then conduct further prioritization of items based on the organization's overall digital workplace priorities and roadmap, available budgets, and other considerations such as IT support staff capacity to introduce or support proposed changes.

Once a plan is established, enhancements should be rolled out in discernable releases or clusters one or more times per year. This allows for adequate user communications and change support before, during, and after all planned changes (see Addendum B for suggested approaches).

Digital Workplace Stewardship Plan Template

Use this template to outline your team or organization's approach to governing and maintaining the entire digital workplace, or specific systems under your purview.

Introduction
The purpose of this plan is to outline the key roles, responsibilities, and approaches related to the stewardship of [COMPANY NAME]'s digital workplace (DW). Tools included in this plan are:

- *List key systems that will be governed in accordance with this plan.*

The objectives of good DW governance are as follows:

1. Preserve the ongoing integrity and relevance of DW tools in the context of the organization's work
2. Establish and maintain clear ownership of DW systems
3. Ensure the continuous improvement of DW systems in accordance with user needs, organizational priorities, and available budgets

It is suggested that this plan be reviewed and revised annually and updated after any major changes to DW systems, ownership, or management.

Key Governance Roles

Stewardship of the [COMPANY NAME] digital workplace requires both strategic-minded leadership to guide the use and improvement of DW systems as well as a focus on the tactical, day-to-day monitoring and management that will keep all systems performing optimally. Specific roles and responsibilities related to the digital workplace fall under the following groups defined in this section:

1. Digital Workplace Leadership Team
2. Digital Workplace Champions
3. IT Support Team

***

Digital Workplace Leadership Team

Executive Sponsor(s):
DW Leader(s):

(Continued)

(Continued)

Leadership Team Responsibilities

1. Serve as the primary system owners for all DW systems and assign varying degrees of system co-ownership and accountability to other departments and individuals as appropriate
2. Maintain an inventory of all IT systems and any useful related data (e.g., owners, date implemented, annual license costs, other costs, etc.)
3. Ensure adequate ongoing support for organization-wide adoption of enhanced DW tools and best practices
4. Continuously monitor and support alignment of DW with organizational strategies and needs
5. Periodically review and discuss DW metrics with stakeholders and leadership to assess system adoption, user satisfaction, and progress toward stated digital transformation goals and objectives
6. Make recommendations and/or produce guidance regarding departmental responsibilities and staff-time allocations for systems and features that they "own" or heavily support
7. Coordinate cross-organizational planning, budgeting, and prioritization of DW enhancements and changes
8. Maintain the integrity of the DW by vetting proposed system modifications, new system purchases/deployments, and configuration changes to ensure they are in alignment with the digital transformation roadmap and system selection criteria (see Addendum A for suggested system selection criteria)

DW Champions: [CHAMPIONS GROUP NAME]

Membership: [GROUP NAME] members should represent a cross-section of the organization, primarily at sub-management level, representing all distinct departments or units. Membership can rotate but it is suggested that members be active for at least a one-year term.

Group Life Span and Meeting Cadence: Ideally the champions group will exist in perpetuity, because there will always be a need to have an engaged group of stakeholders supporting and feeding into the success of the evolving DW. During less active periods, the group could meet less frequently (e.g. quarterly) as opposed to biweekly or monthly during periods of active implementation or rollout of DW tools.

Champion Roles

1. Collect and share their team's perspectives on DW tools
2. Stay informed about DW-related projects and activities
3. Provide input and feedback at critical stages of DW tool design, implementation, and rollout
4. Provide feedback and suggestions on new or existing DW governance policies and processes
5. Share updates on DW plans and changes with their respective teams
6. Serve as advocates and role models for new ways of working supported by DW tools

IT Support Team

IT support staff should be fully invested in the long-term success of the DW and be well equipped to support users to fully adopt and take advantage of all DW tools. IT staff should proactively support and educate users on key system features and functionality while keeping up with the latest developments and updates in key applications and pursuing continuing education in system administration.

(Continued)

(Continued)

IT Support Team Roles (Specifically Related to the Digital Workplace)

1. Provide tier 1 user support and light user education for all DW tools
2. Document (and routinely update) optimal configuration of DW tools to support consistent setup of new machines
3. Set up new machines in accordance with DW configuration guidelines
4. Orient new hires around access and optimal use of DW tools
5. Be on the lookout for emergence of "shadow IT" (i.e. unsanctioned) systems and help users transition to official systems through regular education and user support
6. Run a light change management process around periodic system changes and updates (see Addendum B for a suggested change management process)
7. Maintain a log of user DW-related support issues and routinely (suggest monthly) review as a team to identify any recurring issues needing further attention
8. Enter all user requests for new DW functionality or use cases in a user request backlog for periodic team review (suggest quarterly)
9. Routinely audit system usage and access and report findings to DW Leadership Team

Addendum A: New System Selection Criteria

The following are suggested high-level criteria for the selection of any new systems that will integrate with or form part of the Digital Workplace:

1. User stories and functional requirements should be adequately scoped and documented *before* system selection and configuration, in consultation with representatives from all anticipated user groups.

2. Systems should be cloud-based, wherever possible, to limit the maintenance burden on IT resources and maximize the potential for integration with other DW tools.

3. Systems should, where required, be selected based on whether they are compatible or integrate with existing systems.

4. Systems should support most or all core functionality for staff working remotely, without requiring the use of a remote desktop utility.

5. Systems should be user-friendly, supporting use by those with limited IT skills, and allowing for in-house configuration and management.

6. Where appropriate, systems should satisfy the needs of both part-time and full-time staff.

7. Only systems from an established software provider that can demonstrate financial solvency and a documented track record with similar organizations should be considered.

8. New systems should represent an improvement over the systems they are replacing (if any) in one or more of the following ways: (1) simplification of system architecture through reduction of and/or integration with existing systems, (2) cost savings in terms of licensing and/or maintenance, (3) alignment with strategic priorities, (4) ability to address critical gaps in features or functionality that cannot be achieved through enhancements or add-ons to existing systems.

Addendum B: Change Management for DW System Updates

The following process is recommended for the introduction of any *major* DW system updates or changes that will result in a noticeable impact on the end-user experience (due to changes in existing functionality or addition of new functionality):

1. Cluster communication about all planned and anticipated DW changes and enhancements (both those

(Continued)

(Continued)

initiated by system owners and scheduled/automatic software updates and releases) into scheduled internal "releases." Releases should happen no more than once per quarter.

2. **Maintain a calendar of planned "releases"** and make that calendar available on the IT's intranet support page or other org-wide communication channel. (Note: For late-breaking or rolling software updates, change communication can take place at regular intervals once a critical mass of changes has occurred. This will support greater clarity in user communication and help to avoid change fatigue.)

3. **Prepare training and support materials** as needed that cover new or changed features and functionality in the upcoming release. Consider one-pagers, short videos, or other concise delivery methods and load them to a centrally accessible and high-visibility location prior to release date.

4. **Send advanced notice of changes to all users** one week before release date (two weeks before if changes require any advance preparation by users) via all-staff announcement. Communication should be a concise list of changes written in friendly, non-IT language.

5. **Send follow-up announcement with links to related support documentation** (if warranted) on day of release via all-staff announcement.

6. **Check in with [CHAMPION GROUP NAME] members two to three weeks after the release** to determine whether there have been any related disruptions and whether any additional user training and support is needed.

Your Assignment

- ◆ Using the template provided, create a Digital Workplace Stewardship Plan that is reflective of your organization's needs. As you socialize the idea of digital workplace stewardship among those that you will need support from, emphasize that this is a relatively minor investment of staff time that will serve to preserve, and potentially multiply, the overall investment in the digital transformation effort. Just like an expensive car, the improved digital workplace is a valuable asset that needs care and maintenance to maintain its value. While people may initially be hesitant to offer their time to be part of this group, trust that they will quickly see the value and importance of this level of cross-organizational technology stewardship that goes far beyond the typical role of IT. This group should exist in perpetuity because there will always be a need for the organization to inform the evolving role of technology in supporting the organization's continued health and competitiveness.

CHAPTER 13

Measuring and Improving

The old saying "You get what you measure" certainly applies to the digital workplace. While it may seem obvious that organizations should regularly monitor and measure the performance of their key business systems, this is seldomly done. The metrics you develop during this step will be critical for measuring and communicating the success of the digital transformation effort and what follows, while also making it easier to detect and proactively address issues that could place your organization's technology-related investments at risk.

Now is the perfect time to reflect on the reasons why the organization decided to invest in the digital transformation effort. Think about the processes, behaviors, and technological capabilities that were deemed critical for achieving certain business outcomes. While organizations may use standard methods to measure the adoption and ROI of their digital tools, the story that you tell using these metrics should uniquely reflect the goals, values, and impacts that your organization values most. There is no one-size-fits-all solution to monitoring, measuring, and reporting on the health of the digital workplace. Your work is to define a set of metrics that, taken together, will tell a rich story about how technology is being used in your organization, how well it's performing, and how satisfied and adept people are in using it.

Here are a few best practices to keep in mind.

A good measurement approach includes both *leading* and *lagging* indicators. Leading indicators are metrics that help predict or are a precondition to achieving certain outcomes. Lagging indicators demonstrate that an outcome has already been realized.

When it comes to decisions about what to measure, more is not necessarily better. In fact, the opposite is generally true. Only collect metrics that you intend to use; this will cut down on the time and effort needed to collect and report on them. You can determine what is most important by defining the key questions you will want to answer, and then deciding which metrics and other supplementary information will be needed to tell a clear and convincing story about the state of the digital enterprise.

Collect, analyze, and interpret data at frequent intervals. Routine data collection ensures that you will gather and use information in close to real time. This allows you to detect and react to positive or negative trends as they emerge, rather than several months or years later. Analyzing and interpreting the data close in time to the events driving it will support clear and contextualized sensemaking. No one will remember six months later that one or more key events were perhaps driving observed trends. Without a contextual analysis of what the numbers are telling you, the numbers themselves will only tell part of the story.

■ ■ ■

Use the Digital Workplace Measurement and Reporting Guide that follows to help define an appropriate set of metrics that you or others will use to monitor the overall health of the digital workplace or the subset of tools you are interested in. Be realistic about what you can measure. Every system generates some metrics around usage frequency and other user behaviors but might not give you much insight into specifically how people are using the system. Even with access to detailed system-generated analytics, you'll still need a way to collect user feedback and self-reported measures of satisfaction.

Surveys can be a great tool here, when used sparingly, for collecting more detailed information from users. As an added benefit, this type of outreach can help demonstrate that you are really listening and responding to what users have to say.

Digital Workplace Measurement and Reporting Guide

Use this guide to help develop an approach to monitoring, measuring, and reporting on the health of your digital workplace.

Most modern business applications include native analytics and reports that provide a quick read on usage levels and basic activity types. In addition to these built-in metrics, system managers can manually or automatically extract custom data sets, making use of third-party analytics tools to create more tailored dashboards and reports, and combining data across multiple systems. Regardless of the approach you choose, I suggest collecting system-generated metrics monthly, with a deeper review each quarter, to detect micro and macro trends and ensure that staff are properly deriving maximum value from their tools.

What to Measure

The success of enterprise technology can be measured in terms of user adoption, business value generation, and user satisfaction. Here are some brief definitions of each concept:

User adoption of a given technology occurs when a user decides to make full use of the technology as the best course of action available. I suggest that you develop a more specific definition of adoption for each business system or group of systems and then use system-generated metrics to gauge what percentage of users have reached your defined adoption threshold. Typical adoption metrics include percentage of staff logging in daily and percentage of staff saving

(Continued)

(Continued)

information or generating outputs from a given system, indicating the desired type and frequency of usage.

Value generation is how selected systems are adding value to an individual's work, the key business functions to which they belong, and the organization as a whole. This data is best collected through surveys or interviews with end representative users.

User satisfaction reflects how happy users are with the performance of a given system. The metric could be as general as one question measuring people's overall satisfaction or a series of more granular questions for each system component. Data is best gathered via surveys and first-person accounts shared in interviews or focus groups.

Table 13.1 provides suggested metrics by category that you should consider including in your digital workplace monitoring and measurement approach. For each metric, I have indicated the method or methods by which they are typically collected. These metrics should be tailored to your needs and likely expanded on based on the specific technology of interest and the overall thrust of the digital transformation initiative.

Table 13.1 Suggested metrics to monitor the heath of the digital workplace.

Metric	Type Qual = qualitative Quant = quantitative	Collection frequency	Collection method(s) S = Survey SG = System Generated
Adoption metrics			
% Active users	Quant	Monthly	SG
User activity (e.g. new content/ data generated or shared)	Quant	Monthly	SG
Most frequently visited/used content or components	Quant	Monthly	SG

Metric	Type Qual = qualitative Quant = quantitative	Collection frequency	Collection method(s) S = Survey SG = System Generated
Content/data volume by type	Quant	Monthly or Quarterly	SG
Access by device/ location (e.g. desktop vs. mobile, home vs. office)	Quant	Monthly or Quarterly	SG
Value generation			
User level of trust that system content/data is reliable	Quant	Semi-annually or annually	S
Features and functionality most helpful to a user's work	Quant	Semi-annually or annually	S
Average time needed to perform a task or find needed content/data	Quant	Semi-annually or annually	S
Estimated time savings compared to previous version or system	Quant	One-time, three to six months post-launch/ enhancement	S
Number of system-related help desk tickets and time to resolve (compared to previous version or system)	Quant	One-time, three to six months post-launch/ enhancement for comparison, then quarterly thereafter	SG

(Continued)

(Continued)

Metric	Type Qual = qualitative Quant = quantitative	Collection frequency	Collection method(s) S = Survey SG = System Generated
Types and frequency of desired additional training or support	Qual	Semi-annually or annually	S
User satisfaction			
Overall satisfaction with system and/ or individual components	Quant	Annually	S
Ease of use	Quant	Annually	S
Rating of most/ least helpful features	Quant	Annually	S
Suggested system changes/ improvements	Qual	Annually	S

Once you have a handle on the metrics, it's time to think about how you'll use them. In fact, it's best if you decide how you'll want to use them *before* you finalize your measurement approach. As I mentioned earlier, it is always tempting to collect as much data as possible, but in the end, only the data that gets communicated and used is really worth the effort.

Read the following section, "How to Engage Your Audience with Data," for inspiration on ways to captivate your audience with metrics-driven stories. For the audiences with whom you'll be sharing this information, a bulleted list of statistics on a slide is probably not going to cut it. This is especially true if you need to prove the value of recent investments with organizational leaders or promote increased adoption among end users.

After making a big investment in the digital workplace, the question on everyone's mind, from the CFO down to the IT help desk specialist, is "Was it worth it?" The value of new or reconfigured technology isn't realized on launch day. It takes time for this value to become widely visible to the organization. Hence the need for accurate, clear, and compelling data-driven stories that provide an insider's view of trends and successes to those who, unlike you and your collaborators, are not dutifully monitoring the downstream effects of the recent changes.

Going back to the leading and lagging indicators discussed earlier, metrics around user adoption are leading indicators of a system's value. In other words, the value of a system can only be realized if users adopt it as intended. User satisfaction and value generation metrics are lagging indicators. They represent the outcomes you hope to achieve through a successful implementation and rollout of new or reconfigured tools.

In the early days post-implementation, you can use leading indicators to identify where more training and promotion are needed and detect whether the "laggards" group has finally turned the corner. As system usage takes off, use lagging indicators to show how new tools are becoming an established and trusted part of your digital workplace.

How to Engage Your Audience with Data

How do you present digital workplace data – or any data – in a compelling yet accessible way? Dig deeply into the data and determine the story it wants to tell. Then weave together data, context, and insights into a visually compelling narrative that is concise, accessible, and beautiful.

Once you've selected the information you want to present, use a thoughtful design approach to make your visuals clear and easy to understand. Nice aesthetics won't mean anything if they don't help you tell your story. Here's how to utilize layouts, color, and more to generate interest and engagement:

◆ Avoid 3D graphs and busy backgrounds. This extra visual noise makes it harder for the eye to process information.

(Continued)

(Continued)

- ◆ Use iconography as a shorthand for layering in concepts or data differences and provide a visual key so people can easily identify what they're looking at.
- ◆ Use six colors or less that are distinct enough so as not to be confused. Reserve bright colors for data outliers or specific calls to action.
- ◆ Stick to just one font. The general rule of thumb is to use a single font type in up to three sizes.

Using Infographics Effectively

Infographics are a powerful tool for data storytelling, which can increase retention. In fact, one study found that people remember 65% of the information they see in a visual, versus 10% of the information that they hear.[1] So how can you design infographics that will really get people's attention? Here are a few tips:

- ◆ Align colors and visual style with your brand so it will resonate with staff.
- ◆ Select visuals that "do the talking." This means that images you choose should be easily understood, regardless of the audience's familiarity with the data presented or data visualizations in general.
- ◆ Use simple language and avoid the use of analytical or organization jargon.
- ◆ Use plenty of white space between images so the information has room to "breathe."
- ◆ Use templates to get you started. You don't have to be a design genius to create great visuals. Many popular graphics applications have prebuilt infographic templates that you can use as a starting point.

Visualizing Qualitative Data

You likely have qualitative (i.e. text-based) data to share that you collect from staff surveys and interviews. So how can you disseminate this information in a way that gets the main points across?

Data visualization for text-based data can highlight key takeaways while communicating quantitative measures like how many times a word, phrase, or sentiment was mentioned. This can take the form of word clouds, ranking lists, timelines, photos, icons, or featured quotes.

When used strategically (i.e. not overused), word clouds can be an effective communication tool. The trick is to be intentional in the way you collect the qualitative data that you will use as a source. For example, ask interviewers/survey respondents, "What's one word to describe . . ." Word clouds can also be helpful to compare before and after responses when shown side by side.

Another method is to display representative quotes next to quantitative data. If you have a survey, you can share the quantitative metrics and then include a direct quote or two alongside that bring the results to life. You can go further and include headshots or icons to represent the speaker to make it more personal.

In summary, there are tons of great resources online for how to present visually compelling data visualizations and infographics, and an increasing number of tools to make it quick and easy. So why not give it a try? It will match the level of effort and care that you and your team put into the digital transformation project and provides a chance for everyone to become engaged and invested in its long-term success.

Your Assignment

◆ Develop your digital workplace monitoring, measurement, and reporting approach using the information presented in this chapter as a guide. Again, begin by thinking about the questions that are most important for people across the organization, and then consider how best to answer these questions based on readily available data. You may be tempted to go "overboard," defining a variety of custom metrics or reports that will require lots of data manipulation or time-consuming collection methods. Here, as always, I urge you to start simple. Work with what you have as a starting point; you can always develop a more elaborate version of this plan later on. And when you have the first opportunity to present data to your designated audiences, be sure to ask what they would like to see done differently in the future. Let the consumers of this data be your co-designers as the process matures.

Epilogue

Keeping Technology Human

Throughout this book, I have attempted to emphasize the important, albeit sometimes tenuous, relationship between workplace technology and our humanity. It is a delicate dance. Organizations exist, by and large, to be productive and competitive, while humans want to be happy and fulfilled. These motivations can easily be at odds, but I would argue that technology can help to bridge the divide.

When thoughtfully selected and introduced into the organization, enterprise technology can connect us in ways previously unthinkable, bring joy to the most mundane interactions, and free us up to delve deeper into aspects of our work that are often overlooked due to lack of time. Since thoughtfulness is the key here, our tools rarely deliver their full potential. Technology is not at fault here, people are. Shortage of mindfulness in the workplace is a global pandemic. I would suggest that leaders should be measured by how much the people within their organizations are thriving, not just how much the bank accounts of their investors are growing. Perhaps this is naïve thinking, but I dare us all to dream big. The future health of our societies is at stake.

Where, then, do we go from here, given that technology will only grow in importance, businesses will continue to be profit-driven and risk averse, and humans will continue to be human? This book is by no means a complete solution to these woes. But the perspectives and methods I have shared can certainly help us move past the awkward teenage phase that we are presently experiencing vis-à-vis our relationship with digital tools.

As AI looms large in every area of our lives, it raises important questions about the role technology will play in the near future. Many believe these tools could one day supersede humans, rendering us unemployable, powerless, or worse. I choose to think differently.

185

We have stood in stupefied awe of digital technology for more than half a century. Despite our daily interactions and regardless of our level of knowledge, there is still something sacred, magical, and slightly threatening about these constantly evolving tools. How, then, do we progress beyond the teenage infatuation phase and reach a level of maturity that allows us to exert control over how, and how much, technology dictates the way we live and work? Is it possible to imagine a world in which technology is put to work to vastly improve the quality of our lives while freeing us up to become more human, rather than less so?

These are complicated questions with even more complicated answers. But I'd like to encourage you – now that you have a new-found sense of control over the workplace technology that is hope-fully playing a more harmonious and supportive role within your organization – to consider this possibility. What would true digital maturity and mastery look like in your life, at your organization, in your society? And can we get there before the false gods of zeros and ones take us down a path that befits a careless adolescent uncon-cerned with the consequences of their infatuation?

Let's tread mindfully, and with fully expressed humanity, on the road ahead.

APPENDIX A

Digital Workplace Maturity Assessment

A ssessing the maturity of your digital workplace is an important first step in understanding the current state of your digital tools and highlighting which changes may have the greatest impact. The high-level analysis provided by this assessment is designed to serve as a starting point for investigating the more specific technology-related needs and gaps that exist at your organization.

Keep in mind that the practice of digital workplace design also requires a deep understanding of how people work, their user experience, and the processes that drive their use of different tools. While that level of detail is beyond the scope of this assessment, I hope the results will serve as a useful starting point for your journey toward digital workplace transformation.

Instructions: Please choose the answer that most closely describes your organization from the choices listed. When completed, tally the scores corresponding to each answer (shown in parentheses) and refer to the corresponding analysis for your scores provided at the end of the assessment.

Part 1: Communication

How is email used in your organization?
◆ Email is the primary mode of internal communication (e.g. all-staff messages, document sharing, discussion threads). (1 point)
◆ Email is used frequently for internal communication. (2 points)
◆ Email is occasionally used for internal communication. (3 points)
◆ Email is never or almost never used for internal communication. (4 points)

How are other (non-email) real-time communication tools used in your organization?
◆ We have many different tools and there is little consistency around how and when they're used. (1 point)
◆ We have many different tools and there is some consistency around how and when they're used. (2 points)
◆ We have a few different tools and there is generally a shared understanding about how and when to use them. (3 points)
◆ We have one or more official tools and there are clear guidelines about how and when to use them. (4 points)

How do staff in your organization utilize your corporate intranet?
◆ There is no corporate intranet, or it exists but is not actively used and/or updated. (1 point)
◆ There is a corporate intranet, but it's mainly a static repository of content with limited to no communication features (news, staff directory, etc.). (2 points)
◆ There is a corporate intranet with rich internal communication features and it is used frequently/increasingly by the majority of staff; it is not well integrated with other systems/tools. (3 points)
◆ There is a corporate intranet with rich internal communication features that is used by the vast majority of staff; it's considered the place to go for company news, finding content and people, and is well integrated with other systems/tools. (4 points)

Section Score = [your total] out of 12 points

Part 2: Content and Collaboration

How is content stored within your organization?

◆ Content is stored in a variety of places/tools; it's unclear what to store where. (1 point)

◆ Content is stored in a variety of places/tools; guidelines are in place for what to store where but are not always followed. (2 points)

◆ Content is stored on one or two platforms; guidelines are in place for what to store where and are followed by most staff. (3 points)

◆ Most content is stored on a single platform; platform is well integrated with systems that produce content. (4 points)

How do staff in your organization search for content across platforms and departments?

◆ There's no way to search for content across different storage platforms; search performance of individual platforms is very poor. (1 point)

◆ There is some ability to search for content across different storage platforms but results are not always reliable; search performance of individual platforms is good. (2 points)

◆ Search performance is very good; it is easy and fast to find content stored across different platforms. (3 points)

◆ Search performance is excellent and includes filters and intelligent ranking that orders results based on user characteristics. (4 points)

How do staff in your organization collaborate on files internally for review or co-authoring?

◆ File sharing for review or co-authoring is solely or mostly via email attachments. (1 point)

◆ Sharing files is done primarily through email but usually via links rather than attachments; other collaboration tools are available and used by some staff but not in a consistent way. (2 points)

◆ Sharing files is done primarily outside of email using a mix of tools with little consistency. (3 points)

- Sharing files is done primarily from within one or a few official platforms where most files are stored, and these practices are generally consistent across the organization. (4 points)

How do staff in your organization collaborate on files externally for review or co-authoring?

- File sharing for review or co-authoring is solely or mostly via email attachments. (1 point)
- Sharing files is done primarily through email but usually via links rather than attachments; other collaboration tools are available and used by some staff but not in a consistent way. (2 points)
- Sharing files is done primarily outside of email using a mix of tools with little consistency. (3 points)
- Sharing files is done primarily from within one or a few official platforms where most files are stored, and these practices are generally consistent across the organization. (4 points)

How is document retention and content life cycle management handled within your content management system(s)?

- There are no explicit policies around document retention or content life cycle management, and content owners perform operations manually in an inconsistent manner. (1 point)
- Policies are in place around document retention and/or content life cycle management, but content owners must perform operations manually and do so in an inconsistent manner. (2 points)
- Policies are in place around document retention and/or content life cycle management and are embedded within some/all of our content management systems; some of these operations are automated and consistent across the organization. (3 points)
- Policies are in place around document retention and/or content life cycle management and are embedded within all content management systems; most or all of these operations are automated and consistent across the organization. (4 points)

Section Score = [your total] out of 20 points

Part 3: Data and Information Management

What is the current state of understanding and/or documentation regarding business-critical data residing in your organization's data systems?

◆ There is no central data model defining business-critical data objects or the relationships between them.

◆ There have been some efforts to define business-critical data objects and the relationships between them, but it is limited to specific systems or departments.

◆ There is a documented enterprise data model defining business-critical data objects and the relationships between them, but it is outdated and/or limited in scope.

◆ There is a comprehensive enterprise data model, updated frequently, defining business-critical data objects and the relationships between them; this model informs the design of our data management systems.

How is data stored in your organization?

◆ Data is stored in a variety of places/systems, including static spreadsheets; there is significant overlap and/or duplication of data and widespread concerns about data quality.

◆ Data is centralized in one or more key systems and use of spreadsheets for this purpose is rare; there is some overlap and/or duplication of data and some concerns about data quality.

◆ Data is centralized in one or more key systems and use of spreadsheets for this purpose has been eliminated; there is very limited overlap and/or duplication of data and limited concerns about data quality.

◆ Data is stored in one or more centralized systems that are well integrated and support easy search and discovery based; each data object has only a single source of truth, and confidence in data quality is generally high.

How is data analyzed in your organization?

◆ All or most analysis is performed manually by exporting data from one or more systems; analytics tools are difficult to use without significant training.

192 Digital Workplace Maturity Assessment

- Most analysis is performed manually by exporting data from one or more systems; standard (automated or manual) reports are available but analytics tools are somewhat difficult to use.
- Most analytics are produced via standard automated and manual reports and automated dashboards; analytics tools are relatively easy to use with minimal training.
- Analytics are mostly or fully automated with tools built in or tightly integrated with our data management systems.

Section Score = [your total] out of 12 points

Part 4: Security

Which of the following best describes your organization's approach to data and information security?
- It is mostly reactive; we have some systems and tools in place, but they often make it harder to collaborate; unofficial workarounds are common.
- We have begun to do more to make secure access to our systems more user friendly but it is inconsistent across the organization; security feels like it is hindering us more than helping us.
- Our security systems and protocols allow us to work efficiently but there is limited visibility into what is going on "behind the scenes."
- Our security systems and protocols allow us to work efficiently and provide ways for the end user to contribute to decreasing risk.

Section Score = [your total] out of 4 points

Part 5: Cross-Cutting

How is technology selected at your organization?
- There are no standard criteria or roadmaps that drive how workplace technology is selected.

- There are some system-specific criteria or roadmaps that drive how workplace technology is selected.
- Standard criteria or roadmaps drive selection of most workplace technology.
- There is a comprehensive, frequently updated master plan or roadmap that drives how workplace technology is selected.

Is there a designated governing body responsible for technology strategy at your organization?
- There is no cross-functional decision body driving our technology strategy.
- There is a cross-functional decision body driving our technology strategy but they don't review all major technology decisions.
- There is a cross-functional decision body driving our technology strategy but they don't own or support a digital workplace vision or roadmap.
- There is a cross-functional decision body driving our technology strategy that sets the policies and priorities for digital workplace design and roadmap development.

How, if at all, are AI capabilities being introduced within your enterprise systems?
- We have not begun introducing any AI capabilities and/or plan to do so in the near future but no policies currently exist to guide its use. (1 point)
- We have or are developing policies around use of AI and plan to introduce it into one or more systems in the near future. (2 points)
- We have policies around use of AI and are starting to introduce it into one or more systems. (3 points)
- We have policies around use of AI and have fully implemented it in one or more systems. (4 points)

Section Score = [your total] out of 12 points

Interpreting Your Results
Scoring Method

ANALYSIS BY CATEGORY: COMMUNICATION

Section score	Overview	Recommendations
4–6	It may seem like your organization is seriously behind, but there's no need to be discouraged. You have a great opportunity to define and realize a vision for a truly connected organization.	As you investigate user needs in this area, try to define specific communication "use cases," or actions that people are trying to perform that are particularly challenging within the current environment. Focus on areas where critical capabilities are not readily available to those who need them. After hearing their challenges, ask people to describe how they would ideally like to communicate and with whom, regardless of current toolsets.

If email is used for most communication despite other options being available, explore why people are reverting to email. If the response is something like "It's just easier," try to get specifics on what people are finding challenging about email alternatives. |
| 7–9 | Efforts to streamline communication are beginning to pay off. At this stage, it's important to define a clear vision for the future that everyone can get behind. This vision should make clear how different types of staff will benefit from the planned changes. | Chances are there is still a lot of ad hoc usage of different communication tools. Aim to provide clear guidance on what tools to use for typical use cases. Guidance covering specific staff roles and/or business processes is especially useful. This is also a good time to start consolidating or standardizing these tools as part of a well-designed user experience, to help alleviate tool overload and user confusion.

Explore ways to increase usage and functionality of your available communication tools. Are they salvageable or do they need to me reimagined or replaced to serve people's needs and work styles? You'll want to gather quite a bit of information from current and potential users at this stage. While this will take some time, it's far better than taking a hurried, quick-fix approach that doesn't resolve underlying issues. |

Section score	Overview	Recommendations
10–12	Given your high level of maturity, it's time to take stock of what's working and not working and adjust as needed. You'll also want to make sure that you have built-in processes for continuous improvement as staff communication needs and related technology continue to evolve.	Focus on what's working and provide adequate support for any late adopters to join the mainstream communication practices in your organization. Your system(s) in this area should be producing rich metrics, so be sure to collect, analyze, and report out frequently to encourage thoughtful conversation with all those actively supporting this aspect of the digital workplace. You may want to investigate pockets of resistance to adoption that could represent unmet user needs. It's never too late to build in additional features or functionality that will bring late adopters fully on board.

ANALYSIS BY CATEGORY: CONTENT AND COLLABORATION

Average score	Overview	Recommendations
5–9	Chances are that staff are frustrated from struggles with their content and collaboration tools. Focus on alleviating the biggest pain points as quickly as possible to build support for future changes.	Start by taking an inventory of critical content across the organization and where it resides. Flag instances where outdated content is cluttering frequently searched systems or where duplicate content and/or unsanctioned systems are rampant. Seek to deeply understand the different user behaviors that are driving the current level of disorganization. It may be that technology is not the main culprit, so be on the lookout for hoarding, overly restrictive permissions, and general lack of content management best practices.
10–15	Some of the technology needed for more robust content management and collaboration is likely already in place but user behavior may still be a barrier. Look for ways to promote consistent use of available tools and make sure they're configured to support the best possible user experience.	Despite not having the latest and greatest search capabilities, there are likely some steps you can take to optimize search performance. If possible, gather data on the most popular, as well as unsuccessful, searches in your primary systems of record, and look for ways to push the most relevant content to the top of the results list. Low adoption of newer, improved content and collaboration tools may be due to users' lack of knowledge around system capabilities or mistrust of system stability or security. Randomly survey or talk to different user types to uncover points of resistance, and then craft support materials and messaging that address user concerns.
16–20	You've got great too s in place and user adoption is strong. You can now shift your focus to system enhancements based on user feedback and elimination of legacy systems that may still house content needing to be migrated. And of course, never stop promoting usage guidelines and best practices.	Now is a good time to explore how personalization can turn a good user experience around content and collaboration into a great experience. Think about the different personas in your organization and their needs and contexts. You'll want to conduct interviews to understand how they look for, work on, and discover content to drive requirements in this area. Consider examining the current content and collaboration experience. Look for issues that should be addressed quickly, lest they hurt adoption, such as difficulty with multi-author editing or the use of separate platforms for sharing with people outside of the organization. Now is a great time to ensure you don't leave any people – or important use cases – behind.

ANALYSIS BY CATEGORY: DATA AND INFORMATION MANAGEMENT

Average score	Overview	Recommendations
4-6	Accessing data and turning it into useful information is probably painful and time consuming but don't despair. There are some preliminary steps you can take that will ensure you have a rock-solid foundation for needed improvements in this area.	Your primary focus should be on defining a central data model that will drive any system reconfiguration or design moving forward. The good news is that you don't need advanced technology or a big budget to get started. Begin by getting data producers and consumers together to define the most important types of data moving through your organization, where they reside, and the relationships between them.
		If use of spreadsheets for data storage and analysis is a common practice, start creating an inventory of these so that they can be factored into the data model and design of future systems.
7-9	Moving toward a more streamlined approach to managing your data will likely uncover where duplication and overlaps exist between different systems. Make decisions about which system(s) will serve as the single source or truth for each category of business-critical data.	As you begin to implement improved technology to house and analyze your data, you'll want to future-proof your system designs. This involves thinking about how systems will link to or integrate with one another – now and as new tools are rolled out – in a way that provides the best possible user experience and high-quality outputs.
		When you begin designing systems around the needs of your various users, try user journey mapping. Develop journey maps that outline how frequent data consumers as well as more "casual" consumers (i.e. those who would access more meaningful data if they were readily available) might interact with these systems in the course of their work. You may be surprised when these casual data consumers go on to reap significant, unexpected benefits from their reimagined systems.
10-12	You have overcome some of the most significant challenges in digital workplace design. Given how data needs can shift over time, focus now on building future needs into a data systems roadmap that is updated annually.	While you might have all the right tools in place, you'll want to make sure that they're set up to deliver a great user experience. Are you routinely checking in with active users to solicit ideas for changes or enhancements to your data systems?
		Also look outside of your most active data consumers to those who may not be accessing systems as you had expected. What's keeping them away? While your systems should be well integrated at this point, there may still be gaps that are affecting the ease or usefulness of reporting for those who are less well versed in data science.

ANALYSIS BY CATEGORY: SECURITY

Score	Overview	Recommendations
1	Begin by gathering and reviewing all of the organization's information and data security policies and procedures and reviewing them with knowledgeable staff from different parts of the organization, not just IT. This review should help uncover gaps and inconsistencies that may be causing user confusion and unnecessary levels of risk.	If there is no team exclusively devoted to security and compliance, or if that team is comprised solely of IT professionals, consider forming a security and compliance working group. This can help broaden the conversation to include a healthy consideration of business processes and end-user needs. When undertaking the policy and procedure review, involve this group in the discussion and explore possible changes to the organization's security approaches that could decrease risk, improve the user experience, and leverage the capabilities within existing tools.
2–3	Once improvements begin to roll out to end users, set them up for success by providing adequate change management support around key changes in policies or practice. The goal is to empower staff to be your partners in maintaining higher levels of security across the organization.	It may be useful to seek out security champions across the organization that can help model improved ways of working and serve as an early detection system when user behaviors are exposing the organization to higher levels of risk. Security is a two-way street, so those who set and enforce policies should also regularly seek user feedback regarding how these policies are playing out in the "real world." Without routine adjustments and a constant eye on user compliance and satisfactions, even the best policies can quickly lose their strength.
4	With thoughtful and user-centered security policies and practices in place, the work of good communication and promotion of best practices is never done. Celebrate wins and let users do the talking when it comes to sharing what's working in your security environment.	Consider issuing a quarterly or semi-annual security bulletin or webinar focusing on the areas of improvement in your security stack, with firsthand accounts from users where possible. Communicating before-and-after scenarios is always powerful to show how far the organization has come. Remember to tell the story of your organization's journey in terms of how important security is and the ways in which those who set policies are working hard to support the end-user experience while keeping the organization's data secure. Users will empathize with the inherent difficulties in achieving these goals together and hopefully feel compelled to play an active, supporting role.

ANALYSIS BY CATEGORY: CROSS-CUTTING

Average score	Overview	Recommendations
4–6	The first task before you is to build a coalition of willing partners who can help drive the desired changes across the org. Once assembled, this group can begin the important work of establishing a clear vision and guidelines for the work ahead.	A recommended starting point is to form or repurpose an existing governance body that will oversee all aspects of digital workplace design. This should be a cross-cutting group with considerable non-IT representation, especially from departments or divisions that will stand to benefit the most from any changes. Once a governance body is formed, it is highly recommended that you develop guiding principles for the digital workplace design work going forward. These principles should be comprehensive enough to cover all aspects of your design journey, from stakeholder consultation and technology selection to system implementation and rollout.
7–9	While clear processes are starting to form to support a more ordered approach to managing the overall digital workplace experience, there's still much work to do. Focus on the highest-priority needs to make the best use of limited resources.	If you haven't done so already, develop a future-state digital workplace roadmap that reflects anticipated changes to widely used systems – from major upgrades to platform changes. This will be critical to designing the optimal user experience and to ensure that there is close oversight of the selection of any new technology. Once prepared, share the future-state technology map broadly to gather input, specifically soliciting input on what aspects of the map cause concern or leave out important areas of need. Then continue using this map to communicate what's next and how each step in the digital transformation effort will be bringing the organization closer to more complete and well-designed digital enterprise.
10–12	You now have solid processes in place for managing the digital workplace experience and introducing new tools. If you've been mainly occupied with the work at hand, now is a good time to step back and assess what can be improved.	If user-centered design and continuous improvement have not been standard practices when it comes to your enterprise technology, you now have an opportunity to build this capacity within your organization. You'll want to set up some standard procedures for how these practices get integrated within every technology project and may want to enlist external help if this knowledge is not available internally.

Appendix B

Sample Annual State of the Digital Workplace Survey

Use the following survey as a baseline measurement at the outset of the digital transformation project and annually thereafter to assess staff sentiment around the usability and effectiveness of their digital tools. Results can be used to show positive impacts of the digital transformation project and, going forward, to measure and continuously improve the state of the digital workplace.

Part 1: Respondent Information
1. What is your title/role?
2. Which department do you work in
   List departments
3. How long have you worked here?
   a. Less than one year
   b. One to three years
   c. Four to six years
   d. More than six years

Part 2: Digital Workplace Experience
Please answer the following questions based on your personal experience working at [Company Name]. Comments are encouraged to further support your answer.

Note to survey designer: Suggest including an open comments field after each question.

Options: Strongly agree, Agree, Neither agree nor disagree, Disagree, Strongly disagree:

- I can easily perform my daily work activities with the support of our digital tools.
- I trust that the content, information, and data in our internal systems are reliable and up to date.
- I can easily share and work together on content with my organizational colleagues using our digital tools.
- I can easily share and work together on content with people outside the organization using our digital tools.
- I have access to the training, support, and information I need to use my digital tools effectively.
- Our organization does a good job selecting and deploying new technology when needed.
- Our organization's technology, and the processes that support end users, reflects our organizational values.
- I typically spend the following amount of time each day looking for content, information, or data I need to perform my work:
  a. 0–30 minutes
  b. 30–60 minutes
  c. More than 60 minutes
- Which of the following official digital tools do you use regularly? For those that you do use, rate how satisfied or dissatisfied you are with their overall performance.
    List all major business applications used by the majority of staff with the following rating options:
    Highly satisfied, Satisfied, Neither satisfied nor dissatisfied, Dissatisfied, Highly dissatisfied
- Which of the following unofficial tools do you use regularly?
    List known or generally popular unofficial tools and include a write-in option for those not listed.
- Please rate the following technology-related issues in terms of how much they are impacting your day-to-day work.
    List known technology-related issues you believe to be impacting a significant portion of employees. Include a

write-in option so that respondents can add their own issues to the list. Issue examples include system access issues, sharing permissions, slow system performance/crashes, need for work-arounds, difficulty navigating the system.

Response choices are:

High impact, Moderate impact, Low impact, No impact, or Not applicable

- Please share any specific challenges you are having related to our digital workplace that were not covered in the previous questions.

  [Open Answer]

- What is one thing we could change in the next 6–12 months to improve the state of the digital workplace?

  [Open Answer]

Notes

Chapter 1

1. American Psychological Association, "2023 Word in America Survey," n.d., https://www.apa.org/pubs/reports/work-in-america/2023-workplace-health-well-being.
2. Okta, "Businesses at Work 2024," 2024, 33, https://www.okta.com/sites/default/files/2024-04/Okta-2024_Businesses_at_Work.pdf.
3. Better Cloud, "State of SaaSOps 2023," 2023, https://pages.bettercloud.com/rs/719-KZY-706/images/2023-StateofSaaSOps-report-final.pdf.
4. Kweilin Ellingrud, Rahul Gupta, and Julian Salguero, "Building the Vital Skills for the Future of Work in Operations," McKinsey & Company, August 7, 2020, https://www.mckinsey.com/capabilities/operations/our-insights/building-the-vital-skills-for-the-future-of-work-in-operations.
5. Better Cloud, "State of SaaSOps 2023."

Chapter 3

1. Emily Lawson and Colin Price, "The Psychology of Change Management," McKinsey & Company, June 1, 2003, https://www.mckinsey.com/business-functions/organization/our-insights/the-psychology-of-change-management.
2. Flora Cornish, Nancy Breton, Ulises Moreno-Tabarez, et al., "Participatory action research," Nature Reviews Methods Primers 3, no. 1 (2023), 10.1038/s43586-023-00214-1.

Chapter 4

1. "Parkinson's Law," The Economist, July 10, 2020, https://www.economist.com/news/1955/11/19/parkinsons-law.

Chapter 5

1. **Business use case**, a term from software development, is a description of how a business process or system can provide value to a customer or stakeholder. It defines the objectives, requirements, benefits, and risks of a proposed solution, and outlines the steps and interactions involved in delivering it.
2. "Hybrid Workplace Habits & Hangups," n.d. Glean, https://www .glean.com/resources/guides/hybrid-workplace-habits-hangups.
3. **Enterprise search** is a capability that enables users to query multiple sources of data, such as documents, databases, emails, intranets, and websites, and retrieve relevant and comprehensive results. It can be highly useful in environments where content is stored across multiple systems, each with varying search capabilities and performance.

Chapter 10

1. World Design Organization, "User Experience Design," n.d., https://wdo.org/glossary/user-experience-design.

Chapter 11

1. Everett Rogers, Diffusion of Innovations, 4th ed., 1995.
2. Gartner, n.d., "Change Management Communication," https:// www.gartner.com/en/corporate-communications/insights/ change-communication.
3. Cydney Roach, "Trust and the New Employee-Employer Contract," Edelman, May 8, 2019, https://www.edelman.com/research/trust- and-new-employee-employer-contract.

Chapter 13

1. Jason Helbing, Dejan Draschkow, and Melissa L-H Võ, "Search superiority: goal-directed attentional allocation creates more reliable incidental identity and location memory than explicit encoding in naturalistic virtual environments," *Cognition* 196, 104147 (2020), 10.1016/j.cognition.2019.104147.

Acknowledgments

I'd like to thank all the people who were there for me at the most pivotal moments along the way. Special thanks to my lovely husband, business partner, confidante, and best friend, Jeremy, and our brilliant and beloved daughter, Abigail. My parents, Francine and Andrew, who taught me much and gave me unlimited room to grow. My dear friend Loyce Ong'udi, the bravest and boldest woman I know and a true soul sister, along with her family and the entire community of Rabour Village, Kenya. Fred McConnell, for talking me out of quitting grad school in a time of crisis. Ric Marlink, for taking a chance on a young professional and believing she could pull off the impossible. My patient and kind boss, Christian Pitter, who put up with my rebelliousness and accidentally introduced me to the next stage of my career. The inimitable Anna Miller, my first true professional soulmate and co-conspirator in the war of art. Mark Viso and John Whalen, for clearing a path and trusting in me at a critical professional turning point. To my favorite and funniest "IT guys" and gifted collaborators, Mark Reilley and Keith Fleming. Ross Comstock, the fairy godfather of Ideal State and a true visionary in the world of IT. All Ideal State employees, past and present, who deliver heartfelt support and guidance to our amazing clients: Carrie Boron, Lindsay Dahl, Tara Hansen, David Nurse, Michalla Sedano, Fano Endor, Laura Schuck, Caroline Nurse, Joyann Jerriho, Em Beauchamp, and Carmen Brooks. And of course, special thanks to Christina Rudloff at Wiley for her willingness to champion the idea for this book and her cheerful encouragement throughout the process.

About the Author

Sara is CEO of the digital transformation consulting firm Ideal State, which she co-founded in 2016 after a 15-year career in the international health and development sector. She has been a featured speaker at various industry conferences, including KMWorld, APQC, NTEN, and Digital Workplace Experience, on the topics of digital transformation and knowledge management. She holds a master's of public health (MPH) from the University of Washington.

Sara's lifelong passion for writing and communication manifested in a variety of ways over the course of her career, starting with a role within the public affairs department at the newly established Bill & Melinda Gates Foundation in the early 2000s. From there, she continued to combine her diverse talents and deep interest in the African continent while working at organizations on the front lines of the global HIV pandemic.

While serving as senior technical editor for the Elizabeth Glaser Pediatric AIDS Foundation (EGPAF) in 2006, she discovered the practice of knowledge management (KM) and became a certified KM practitioner. Excited by the possibilities of applying KM methods and the latest technology to support learning and continuous improvement in an international NGO working in over 25 countries, Sara spearheaded EGPAF's first-ever institutional KM program.

A perpetual internal change agent, Sara went on to lead highly successful digital transformation initiatives focused on everything from field-level data collection and analysis to global collaboration and innovation. Just prior to co-founding Ideal State, Sara served as KM director for the international NGO Pact, where she led a wide-ranging, high-profile effort to enhance all aspects of Pact's global operations through a more strategic and mindful approach to the selection and rollout of enterprise technology.

As lead strategist for many of Ideal State's client projects, Sara blends the practices of knowledge management, human-centered design, and change management to bring a people-first orientation to every engagement.

Outside of work, Sara enjoys spending time in the great outdoors in her adopted hometown of Santa Fe, New Mexico, together with her husband, Jeremy, and their young daughter, Abigail.

Index

Page numbers followed by *f* and *t* refer to figures and tables, respectively.

Take Control of Your Tech

For resources to support your human-centered digital transformation journey, including:

- Digital Workplace Assessment
- Sample Workplace Surveys
- Templates + Activities
- Media + Podcasts
- Community
- Custom Solutions
- and more..

Visit SaraTeitelman.com